Chic Knits for Young Chicks

Chic Knits for Young Chicks

Sarah Paulin

A LARK/CHAPELLE BOOK

A Division of Sterling Publishing Co., Inc.
New York

A Lark/Chapelle Book

Chapelle, Ltd., Inc.
P.O. Box 9255, Ogden, UT 84409
(801) 621-2777 • (801) 621-2788 Fax
e-mail: chapelle@chapelleltd.com
Web site: www.chapelleltd.com

Created and produced by
Red Lips 4 Courage Communications, Inc.
www.redlips4courage.com
Eileen Cannon Paulin
President
Catherine Risling
Director of Editorial

10 9 8 7 6 5 4 3 2 1

First Edition

Published by Lark Books, a division of
Sterling Publishing Co., Inc.
387 Park Ave. South, New York, NY 10016

Distributed in Canada by Sterling Publishing
c/o Canadian Manda Group, 165 Dufferin St.
Toronto, Ontario, Canada M6K 3H6

Distributed in the United Kingdom by GMC Distribution Services,
Castle Place, 166 High Street, Lewes, East Sussex, England BN7 1XU

Distributed in Australia by Capricorn Link (Australia) Pty. Ltd.
P.O. Box 704, Windsor, NSW 2756, Australia

ISBN 13: 987-1-57990-997-0
ISBN 10: 1-57990-997-3

For information about custom editions, special sales, premium and
corporate purchases, please contact Sterling Special Sales Department
at (800) 805-5489; or e-mail specialsales@sterlingpub.com.

Table of Contents

Introduction.......................6
• Knitting Supplies
• Basic Techniques

CHAPTER 1
Scarves......................34
• Biggy Rib Scarf
• Fuzzy Bunny Scarf
• Skelt Scarf
• Retro Checkered Scarf
• Softee Scarf
• Woven "Braid" Scarf
• Headband Scarf

CHAPTER 2
Shrugs & Ponchos............50
• Continuous Shrug
• Island Poncho
• Cuirass Shrug
• Colinette Shrug
• Summer Shrug

CHAPTER 3
Belts & Caps.....................62
• Trendsetter Belt
• Teen's Hat
• Beanie Cap
• Fall Belt

CHAPTER 4
Warmies...........................74
• Slippers
• Wrist Warmers
• Tube Top/Skirt
• Arm Warmers
• Hand Warmers

CHAPTER 5
Purses & Handbags............88
• Felted Purse
• Felted Tigress Bag
• Felted Mini Purse
• Felted Purse with Handles
• Bag with Pom-Poms
• Evening Bag
• Clutch Purse
• Recycled Yarn Bag
• Karaoke Felted Purse
• Sparkling Purse

CHAPTER 6
Accessories......................112
• I-Pod Cozy
• Sparkling Water Bottle Holder
• Bubbly Water Bottle Holder
• Fuzzy Pillow

CHAPTER 7
Gifts...............................122
• Guy's Hat & Scarf
• Journal Cover
• Baby Blanket
• Thrummed Tea Cozy

Acknowledgments...................134

Metric Equivalency Charts.......134

Index..................................135

Introduction

While I enjoy all kinds of creative projects, knitting is one of my favorites. It's portable, fun, and I can do it with friends. By choosing my own yarns and needle sizes, I make things that are different from anything I've seen before. Knitting lets me express myself and gives me a way to show off my fashion sense.

I first learned how to knit when I was 5 years old. My mother sat with me on a long plane ride and taught me what her grandmother had taught her. She put two long needles in my little hands and a ball of yarn in my lap, and explained the basics.

Like most young girls who knit, I quickly moved on to the scarf craze. Soon my needles were flying—I could knit a scarf in a day and I loved all the different yarns. By then I could sit through learning how to purl and bind off. If my mother wasn't around to answer questions, I'd find a website with instructions or head to my mom's knitting basket for a book.

While scarves are fun to knit and easy to make, you can only have so many. So the next step for me was knitting shrugs and ponchos. As I got better and became more confident, I took on projects like purses and handbags.

I like to share my designs, color choices, and the embellishments that make my projects stand out. And now I'm excited to pick a few of my favorites and share them with you. Feel free to alter patterns, or add or delete adornments. Just remember to have fun knitting your own chic designs!

Sarah Paulin

Knitting Supplies

Yarns

One of the first things you will do is select a yarn or two for your project. There are many different weights, colors, fibers, and textures of yarn available for any knitting project.

If you prefer to knit your project to look exactly like the piece in this book, simply purchase the yarn listed in the instructions. However, if you would like to knit a piece that is uniquely your own, feel free to experiment with another yarn.

Be aware that all yarns are not created equal. You need to choose a yarn that is suited to the pattern you would like to knit. If you have chosen to knit a project that has a decorative pattern such as a seed stitch or a cable, you should stick to a smooth-plied yarn in a solid color. If you are knitting a piece that has a fairly simple pattern such as the stockinette stitch, you can choose from the many fabulous multi-colored and textured yarns that are available today.

Often, a yarn will create varied and surprising effects when you knit it using different techniques. For example, when knitted in the round, variegated yarns will create a striped effect. Do not be afraid to experiment when you are unsure of how a yarn and a pattern will behave together.

Yarn Balls, Skeins & Hanks

Yarns are available in hanks (A), balls (B), and skeins (C). Those yarns you find in balls and skeins are wound and packaged so they are ready to knit, meaning you simply find the end and begin knitting. However, yarns that are sold in looped and twisted hanks require special preparation before you can begin knitting. Undo the twist to find the large loop, then have a friend hold the loop with both hands while you find one end and begin winding it into a ball. Once you have wound all the yarn into a ball, you are ready to get started.

Yarn Weights

Yarns come in many different thicknesses. These are called weights. The weight of a yarn largely determines the gauge, or how many stitches it will take to make up 4" of knitting, and the size of needle you use for working your project. Our chart (page 9) shows the different weights of yarn, the average gauge for each, and the needle size usually used with each weight.

Plies Defined

Yarn is also made up of plies. The number of plies is the number of strands of yarn twisted together. Tightly twisted and multi-plied yarns are generally strong, smooth, and even. A loosely twisted or single-ply yarn will have more loft, softness, and warmth than the tighter-twisted yarn, but the strand will be easier to split with needles.

Although the number of plies is relative to the strength of the yarn, it does not necessarily imply thickness. A yarn with four plies of thin strands can be thinner than a heavier-weight single-ply yarn.

Combining Colors & Textures

Several projects in this book use the technique of combining yarns, or holding multiple strands together and knitting them as one. This is a fun yet unpredictable way to create one-of-a-kind colors and textures.

When you are combining colors, you may wish to study a color wheel. This artist's tool can help you decide whether to use complementary colors (those directly across from each other on the wheel) to create balance and high contrast, or analogous colors (those that are side by side on the wheel) to create a harmonious shift from one color to the next. Be aware when you are using a yarn that has multiple colors that combining it with a yarn that has one or more of the same colors will cause those colors to either fade out of the design or provide contrast for the remaining colors.

As a general rule when combining yarn textures, choose a base yarn that will provide structure for the item and an accent yarn that will add eye-catching effects.

Take time to experiment with a variety of colors, textures, and combinations to see what works and what does not. It is a good idea to make a sample or two first, using the yarns you have chosen. This way you avoid knitting an entire piece only to find you dislike the color and/or texture combination. Experiment with different needle sizes as well. You may find that some textured yarns will perform better when worked on a larger needle than on a smaller one.

Knitting Needles

Knitting needles come in a variety of shapes, sizes, lengths, and materials to suit your project and your knitting style.

Needle Shapes

Knitting needles are available in three basic shapes. There are straight needles, which have a stop at one end and are used for knitting flat pieces (A); circular needles, which consist of two needle ends that are joined by a flexible nylon strand and are used for knitting "in the round" to create a tube (B); and double-pointed needles, which are straight with a point at each end, come in a set of four, and are also used for knitting a tube shape, but on a smaller scale (C).

Needle Sizes

Knitting needles are sized by diameter. The smaller the needle number, the smaller the needle is in diameter and the smaller and tighter the stitch. American sizing of needles is from zero to 15. European needles are sized by their diameter in metric millimeters. The sizes are somewhat equivalent between the two standards for measurement.

Needle Lengths

Just as knitting needles are available in more than one size or diameter, they are also available in more than one length. Straight needles come in lengths from 10" to 16". Circular needles are available in standard lengths of 16", 24", 29", and 36". Double-pointed needles can be found in 5", 7", and 10" lengths.

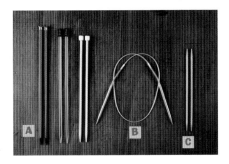

When you are trying to decide which length of needle to use for your project, check the size of your project. It is better to select a needle length that is slightly shorter than the width of the project than to use one that is too long and ends up stretching the knitting. This applies especially when working with circular needles.

Needle Materials

Needles made of aluminum or plastic are easy to find and are fairly inexpensive. However, if you would like to spend a bit more money on your needles, you can also find them in bamboo, wood, and hand-blown glass. Although all of these will stitch the same, each of them will feel different in your hands.

Certain needle types are more suitable for particular projects and yarns. For instance, needles made from dark exotic wood can help you knit a fine, light yarn; the contrast between the two eases the task. Slippery yarns often work best on wood or bamboo, whereas coarser fibers move more effortlessly and seem to knit up more quickly on shiny, nickel-coated aluminum or brass.

Types of Yarn	in Category	Number of Stitches in 4"	US Needle Size
Super Fine	Baby, Fingering, Sock	27-32 sts	1-3
Fine	Sport, Baby	23-26 sts	3-5
Light	DK, Light Worsted	21-24 sts	5-7
Medium	Worsted, Afghan, Aran	16-20 sts	7-9
Chunky	Chunky, Craft, Rug	12-15 sts	9-11
Super Chunky	Bulky, Roving	6-11 sts	11 and up

Other Supplies

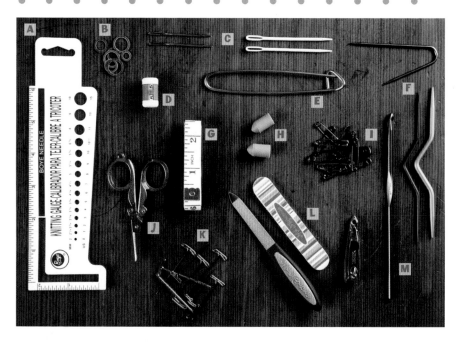

A Gauge ruler/needle sizer

This tool has an L-shaped window you can use to count stitches per inches to find your gauge. It also has graduated holes to help you find the size of any unmarked knitting needles and to determine if one needle marked size 6 is bigger than another needle also marked size 6.

B Stitch markers

A stitch marker is a small ring you slip onto your knitting needle to help keep track of stitches or places in your work that require special attention such as the beginning and end of a repeat. When you come to a stitch marker, slip it from the left-hand needle onto the right-hand needle and continue knitting.

C Tapestry needle

A tapestry needle is used for weaving in yarn ends, sewing knitted pieces together, and embroidery work. This type of needle has a large eye that accommodates the yarn and a blunt point that helps you avoid splitting the yarn on the pieces you are sewing.

D Row counters

Use row counters and markers to help keep track of how many rows you have completed. Place a counter in the first stitch from where you want to count. Continue knitting and periodically stop, count 20 rows, and place another counter. In placing a counter every 20 rows, you will be able to count rows without having to start at the beginning each time.

E Stitch holders

These extra-long safety pins are used for holding stitches that will be worked or finished off later. Stitch holders are available in lengths from 1¾" to 8".

F Cable needles

These elongated crooked or U-shaped double-pointed needles are used for holding stitches while you are working a cable pattern.

G Tape measure

You will need a tape measure marked in inches and centimeters for measuring gauge and checking project length.

H Point protectors

These are small rubber stoppers that you put on the points of your needles when you are not knitting. Not only will they protect the points, but they will also keep your stitches from sliding off the needles between knitting sessions.

I Safety pins

In knitting, safety pins are used in a number of different ways. They are often used as row counters and stitch markers. They are also good for securing dropped stitches and pinning seams.

J Scissors

Scissors are necessary for cutting yarn as you work. Look for a small, portable set that will fit in your knitting bag.

K Blocking pins

These pins have large heads that will not get lost in the weave of the knitted fabric. They are used for pinning a piece in place for blocking and for pinning pieces together for sewing.

L Nail clippers or nail file/ emery board

A hangnail or a broken fingernail can be a nightmare when you are trying to manip-ulate your yarn. Keep at least one of these in your knitting bag.

M Crochet hooks

A crochet hook is used for some finishing work and for recovering dropped stitches. For most projects, a medium-sized crochet hook is best.

Abbreviations

. . . .

BO = bind off

CC = contrast color

CO = cast on

dec = decrease

dpn = double-pointed needles

g = gram(s)

inc = increase

k = knit

k2tog = knit 2 together

kfb = knit in front and back

MC = main color

mm = millimeter(s)

oz = ounce(s)

p = purl

p2tog = purl 2 together

sl st = slip stitch

ssk = slip, slip, knit stitch

st or sts = stitch(es)

st st = stockinette stitch

rev st st = reverse stockinette stitch

Rnd = round

RS = right side

WS = wrong side

yds = yards

yo = yarn over

break = disconnect yarn that is being worked from the skein either by breaking it or cutting it

change to = a change in needle size. Simply place needle holding the work in your left hand and begin working into the stitches as instructed with the new-sized needle in your right hand. Do not slide work off old size and onto new size.

knitwise = insert right-hand needle as if to knit (from front to back and left to right)

purlwise = insert right-hand needle as if to purl (from back to front and right to left)

work even = continue in the specified pattern without increasing or decreasing (using same number of stitches)

Commas, Asterisks, Brackets & Parentheses

There are a few symbols that are consistent in most patterns, including:

- **Commas**—,—indicate the completion of an action. The text written between commas is a single step.
- **Asterisks**—*—indicate the beginning and ending of stitches that will need to be repeated. For example: *K2, p4, repeat from * five times. After knitting two stitches and purling four stitches, you would repeat those stitches five times, equaling six times total that the stitches are worked. Sometimes you will repeat to the end of the row.
- **Brackets**—[ ]—can be used instead of asterisks to indicate repeats. For example: [K4, p6] three times. Here, you would knit four stitches and purl six stitches three times.
- **Parentheses**—( )—are used to indicate alternate information for sizes, stitches, and measurements for projects that can be worked in more than one size. For example: Garment Size: 7 (9, 11), Sts: 18 (24, 32), or Finished Measurement: 24" (28", 36").

Gauge

Your pattern will include a gauge notation (the number of stitches and rows per inch) for the weight of yarn and size of needles required to make the photographed sample.

It is very important to knit your own "gauge swatch" with the yarn you have chosen before starting any project. This way you can see if your tension equals the gauge called for in the pattern.

Knit a square in the pattern or stitches indicated that is five to 10 stitches and five to 10 rows larger than that called for in the pattern's gauge notation. Press the finished square under a damp cloth and allow it to dry. Mark out the stitches indicated for gauge with blocking pins and measure the inches with your tape measure or knitting gauge (above).

If you have too many stitches per inch, you are working too tightly. You need to stitch with less tension or switch to larger needles. Similarly, if you have too few stitches per inch, you are working too loosely. In this case, you need to stitch with greater tension or switch to smaller needles. Always knit a gauge swatch!

Basic Techniques

Knitting is quite easy once you know the basics. There are really only a few stitches that are worked in different combinations to create all the stitch patterns you find in any given piece of knitting. As you are learning new techniques, your knitting will be a bit slow going. But once you have them down, it's simply a matter of finding your own rhythm. When you are in your knitting "groove," you will find that you can knit a pattern of stitches that you know and watch your favorite TV show or even your best friend's soccer game at the same time.

The Basics

Making a Slip Knot

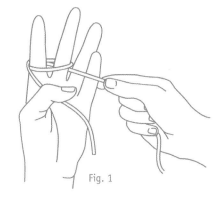

Fig. 1

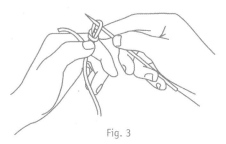

Fig. 3

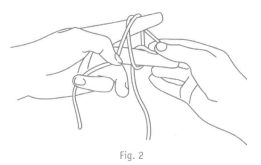

Fig. 2

1. Leaving a long tail (approximately 1" per stitch to be cast on plus an additional 4"–6") on your yarn and, beginning with your left-hand palm facing you, hold the tail end with your left-hand thumb. With your right hand wrap the yarn around your index and middle fingers. (Fig. 1)

2. Pull the working end, or the end that is attached to the ball, through the loop on your fingers, creating a new loop. (Fig. 2)

3. Remove your fingers and pull the tail end of the yarn to tighten the knot. Place the loop on one of your needles and tighten it so that it does not slide off by pulling on the working end. (Fig. 3)

Needle Sizes

US	Metric
0	2mm
1	2¼mm
2	2¾mm
3	3¼mm
4	3½mm
5	3¾mm
6	4mm
7	4½mm
8	5mm
9	5½mm
10	6mm
10½	6½mm
11	8mm
13	9mm
15	10mm

Cast On (CO)

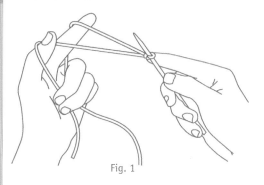

Fig. 1

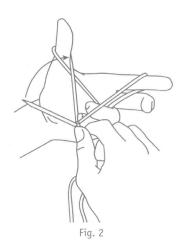

Fig. 2

1. Holding the needle with the slip knot in your right hand, wrap the tail end of the yarn around your left thumb and the working end around your left index finger. Secure both ends with your other fingers in your palm, holding your thumb and index finger in a vertical position and creating a "V" with the yarn. (Fig. 1)

2. Bring the tip of the needle up and under the lower strand of the loop on your thumb. (Fig. 2)

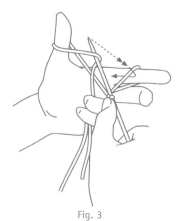

Fig. 3

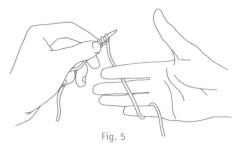

Fig. 5

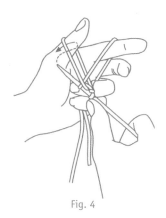

Fig. 4

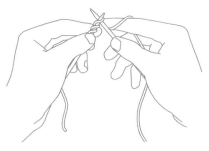

Fig. 6

3 Move the tip of the needle up and over the closest strand of the loop on your index finger and back down through the loop on your thumb. (Fig. 3)

4 Slip the loop off your thumb and pull the tail end of your yarn to tighten the stitch on the needle. (Fig. 4)

5 Return your thumb to the "V" position and repeat Steps 1–4 until you have cast on the required number of stitches.

1 Hold the needle with the cast-on stitches in your left hand with the first stitch approximately 1" from the needle tip, next to your index finger. Wrap the working yarn around your right pinkie finger and weave it up and over your index finger to help maintain yarn tension. (Fig. 5)

2 Position your right index finger approximately 2" from the tip of the right needle and your thumb 1" below that. Gently hold the needle with the rest of your fingers. Your right index finger will control the tension of the yarn. (Fig. 6)

Knit Stitch (k)

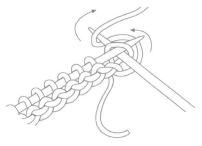

Fig. 1

Fig. 2

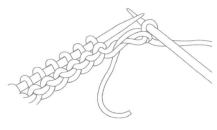

Fig. 3

1 Hold the needle with the cast-on stitches in your left hand. Insert the right needle tip from front to back into the first stitch at the bottom, or back, of the left needle. The yarn should be waiting at the back of the work. With your right index finger, wrap the yarn under, up, and over the right needle. (Fig. 1)

2 Keeping the yarn on the tip of the right needle, draw this loop toward you, through the original stitch on the left needle. Push the right needle up so the new stitch is approximately 1" from the tip. (Fig. 2)

3 Slide the original stitch off the left needle by pulling on the right needle. You now have a knit stitch on the right needle. (Fig. 3)

4 Repeat Steps 1–3 until all the stitches are on the right needle.

Purl Stitch (p)

Fig. 4

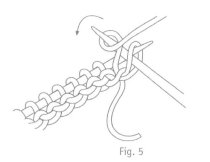

Fig. 5

1 Hold the needle with the cast-on stitches in your left hand. Hold the yarn to the front of the work and in front of the right needle. (Fig. 4)

2 Insert the right needle tip from back to front into the first stitch at the top, or front, of the left needle. Wrap the working yarn up and around the right needle in a counterclockwise direction. (Fig. 5)

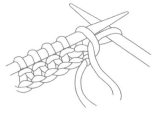

Fig. 6

Fig. 7

3 Draw the yarn backward through the original stitch on the left needle, forming a new stitch on the right needle. Push the right needle up so the new stitch is approximately 1" from the tip. (Fig. 6)

4 Slide the original stitch off the left needle by pulling the right needle toward the back of the work. (Fig. 7)

5 Repeat Steps 1–4 until all the stitches are on the right needle.

Garter Stitch

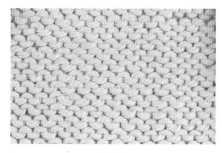

For any number of stitches.
Knit all rows to form the garter stitch. The work is characterized by a pattern of horizontal ridges.

Stockinette Stitch (st st)

For any number of stitches.
Row 1 (RS): Knit.
Row 2: Purl.
Repeat these two rows to form the stockinette stitch.

Reverse Stockinette Stitch (rev st st)

For any number of stitches.
Row 1 (RS): Purl.
Row 2: Knit.
Repeat these two rows to form the reverse stockinette stitch.

Great Idea!
Ask for Help
Most specialty yarn stores have tables where customers gather to knit and learn. If you are stumped and can't figure out a part of your project, stop by for help.

Ribbing

The ribbing technique is used for creating a somewhat elastic, or stretchy, knitted fabric. It is usually worked along the edges of a garment. Ribbing also serves to create a balanced, reversible fabric. Because there is the same number of knit and purl stitches on each side of the fabric, the piece will not curl up like the stockinette stitch does.

K1 p1 Rib Stitch
For any number of stitches.
Knit 1, purl 1 on all rows.

K2 p2 Rib Stitch
For a multiple of 4 stitches.
Knit 2, purl 2 on all rows.

K4 p4 Rib Stitch
For a multiple of 8 stitches.
Knit 4, purl 4 on all rows.

Seed Stitch

For an even number of stitches.
Row 1 (RS): Knit 1, purl 1 to end of row.
Row 2: Purl 1, knit 1 to end of row.
Repeat these two rows to form the seed stitch.

Bind Off (BO)

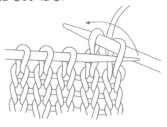

Fig. 1

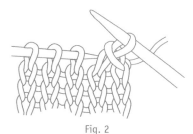

Fig. 2

Binding off is the technique for removing your work from the needles so that your stitches do not unravel.

1 Hold the needle with the work in your left hand. Knit the first 2 stitches on the row. Insert the left needle tip into the first knitted stitch on the right needle. (Fig. 1)

2 Carefully lift this stitch over the second knitted stitch and off the right needle. (Fig. 2)

3 Knit the next stitch off the left needle and lift the previous stitch over the new stitch. Repeat until there is only one stitch left on the right needle.

4 Break the yarn, leaving a 6" tail hanging from the completed work. Slip the last stitch off the needle and thread the end through the loop. Pull snugly to secure.

Bind Off Knitwise

Work the bind-off row entirely with knit stitches regardless of the established pattern.

Bind Off In Pattern

After knitting into the first two stitches to begin the bind off row, work in accordance with the pattern. For example: Continue by knitting 1, then purling 1, etc.

Right Side (RS) vs. Wrong Side (WS)

The right side is the side that will face out when you are wearing the garment. Usually, the knit side is the right side. Similarly, the wrong side is the inside, or underside, of the garment. When you are working the stockinette stitch, the wrong side is the purl side.

Shaping

Shaping is a general term used to indicate the manipulation of stitches, using decreases or increases, to create angled or curved edges in the knitted fabric.

Decrease (dec)

Decreasing is used to help shape your knitting by making it narrower. This book uses the following techniques for decreasing stitches: Knit 2 Together (k2tog), Purl 2 Together (p2tog), Slip Stitch (sl st), and Slip, Slip, Knit Stitch (ssk).

Knit 2 Together (k2tog)

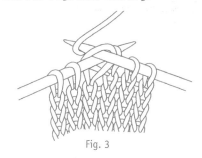

Fig. 3

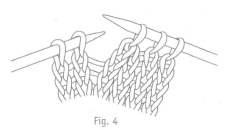

Fig. 4

1 To work this decrease, insert the right needle from front to back into the next 2 stitches on the left needle, working into the second stitch first, then the first stitch. The yarn should be waiting at the back. (Fig. 3)

2 Knit both stitches together as one, and slide the resulting decreased stitch onto the right needle. (Fig. 4)

Purl 2 Together (p2tog)

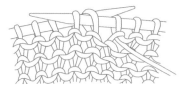

Fig. 1

1 With the yarn in front, insert the right needle into the front of the next 2 stitches, purl them both together as one and slide this decreased stitch onto the right needle. (Fig. 1)

Slip Stitch (sl st)

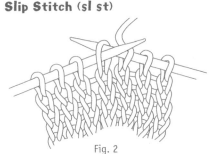

Fig. 2

1 Insert the right needle purlwise into the stitch on the left needle and slip the stitch onto the right needle without knitting it or changing its orientation. (Fig. 2)

Slip, Slip, Knit Stitch (ssk)

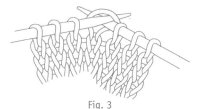

Fig. 3

1 Insert the right needle knitwise into the next 2 stitches on the left needle and slip the stitches onto the right needle without knitting them. (Fig. 3)

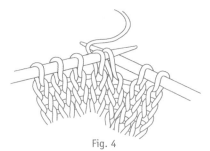

Fig. 4

2 Insert the left needle into the front of the loops of these 2 stitches. (Fig. 4)

3 Knit the 2 stitches together.

Increase (inc)

Increasing is used to help shape your knitting by making it wider. This book uses the following technique for increasing, or adding, stitches: Knit into the Front & Back (kfb).

Knit into the Front & Back (kfb)

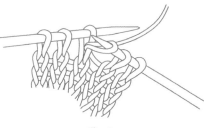

Fig. 5

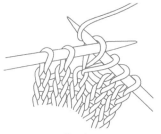

Fig. 6

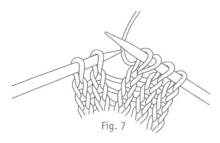

Fig. 7

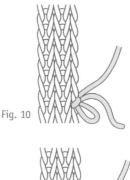

Fig. 10

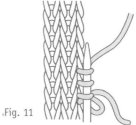

Fig. 11

1. With the right side of the work toward you, begin knitting into the stitch (into the front). Pull the new stitch through, but do not slide the original stitch off the left needle. (Fig. 5)

2. Knit through the back of the same original stitch. (Fig. 6)

3. Slide the stitch off the left needle, onto the right needle. (Fig. 7)

Yarn Over (yo)

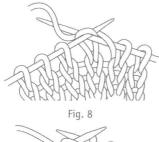

Fig. 8

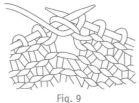

Fig. 9

A yarn over creates a tiny hole in the knitting.

1. Bring your yarn to the front of the work. Insert the right needle from front to back into the next stitch. Wrap the yarn over and behind the right needle and continue knitting normally. (Fig. 8)

2. In the next row, on the wrong side of the work, purl the yarn over the loop. (Fig. 9)

1. With the right side of the work toward you, temporarily anchor a new ball of yarn to the right edge of your knitting by tying it on in a half knot (you can untie it later). (Fig. 10)

2. Using a knitting needle, insert the needle tip between the running strands of the first two stitches along a vertical edge (or into the first stitch, which is the top of the "V" just below the bound off edge on a horizontal edge). Catch the yarn waiting underneath and pull it through the stitch, creating a loop. Place the loop on the needle—one stitch picked up. Move to the next stitch and continue in this manner until the required number of stitches have been picked up. (Fig. 11)

3. These picked up stitches can now be worked as directed in the pattern. **Note:** It is important to evenly space a given number of stitches in an area of knitting—especially along a vertical edge. To do this, divide the length into four sections and pick up one quarter of the total number of required stitches in the first section. You may need to skip a running strand every few stitches to make the number come out evenly spaced.

Knit-On Cast On

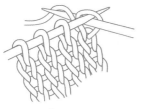

Fig. 1

Fig. 2

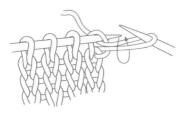

Fig. 3

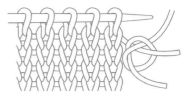

Fig. 4

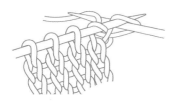

Fig. 5

1 With the right side of the work toward you, insert the right needle into the first stitch and draw out a loop, pulling it a bit longer than normal. (Fig. 1)

2 Insert the left needle through the loop from the front and below. (Fig. 2)

3 Slip the new loop onto the left needle and pull the stitch tightly. Do not remove the right needle. (Fig. 3)

4 Draw out another loop and repeat Steps 2–3 until you have knit on the required number of cast-on stitches. (Figs. 4–5)

Joining a New Yarn

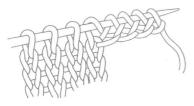

Fig. 6

Join a new yarn when you are working with more than one ball of yarn or when you are working with more than one color. It is best to join a new yarn at the beginning of a row to avoid having a knot that will show through your work or come undone, leaving a hole. Joining at the beginning of the row also makes it easier to weave in ends after you have finished knitting your project.

1 At the beginning of the row, start knitting with the new yarn, leaving a 4" tail. Tie the old and new yarns together in a loose knot close to the work. Continue knitting with the new yarn. (Fig. 6)

Adding a New Yarn

Add a new yarn when you are currently working with one yarn and want to begin working two yarns together as one to add color or texture to the knitted fabric.

1 At the beginning of the row, start knitting with the old yarn and the new yarn held together as one, leaving a 4" tail on the new yarn. Temporarily anchor the new yarn to the right edge of your knitting by tying it on in a half knot. Continue knitting the two yarns as one.

Change To (changing yarns)

This technique is used when you want to change colors in your knitting as for striping.

1 At the beginning of the row, start knitting with the new yarn, leaving a 4" tail. Tie the old and new yarns together in a loose knot close to the work. Continue knitting with the new yarn.

Needle Notes:
Changing Yarns

Whenever you change colors of yarn, knit the first stitch of the round with both MC and CC, and then complete the round as normal. This will create smoother stripes. When changing to a new color stripe, carry the yarn up the inside of the work. Make certain to leave enough slack so that the piece will lay flat. This will reduce the number of ends to weave in.

Carry Yarn Up (striping)

When you are knitting narrow stripes and changing colors (Change To) often, you can use the Carry Yarn Up technique to avoid breaking yarns and to make sure the needed color is always at hand.

Fig. 7

Fig. 8

1 When you change to a different color, drop the old yarn and begin knitting with the new color. Work the rows as directed, carrying the old yarn loosely up the side of your work until it is time to drop the new color and resume knitting with the old. (Fig. 7) If you are carrying the yarn for more than two rows, twist the colors every other row. (Fig. 8)

Knitting in the Round

Knitting in the round is used when you want to create seamless, tube-shaped projects such as the hats and water bottle holders featured in this book.

This technique is worked on circular needles for larger projects and double-pointed needles for smaller projects or sections of projects. When you are choosing a needle length for your project, remember that you can always squeeze the stitches together on a needle that is somewhat shorter, but you cannot stretch out the work on a needle that is too long—select a needle that is shorter than the circumference of your project.

After casting on, the stitches are joined in a circle and the progression is worked in "rounds" instead of rows. The biggest difference between knitting in the round and working back and forth in rows is that you do not have to turn the work when you are working in rounds. Because the right side of the work is always facing you, you do not need to change knit stitches to purl stitches on the wrong side of the work.

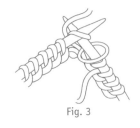

Fig. 3

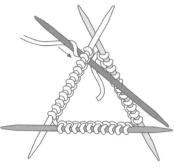

Fig. 4

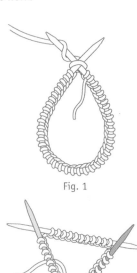

Fig. 1

Fig. 2

1. Whether you are using circular or double-pointed needles, cast on the required number of stitches all on one needle. (Fig. 1) If you are using double-pointed needles, evenly divide the cast-on stitches between three or four needles by sliding the stitches over from either end, leaving one needle to knit with. (Fig. 2) Check the cast-on stitches to make certain they are not twisted on the needles—the cast-on edge should be at the bottom of the needles.

2. Place a marker after the last cast-on stitch. (Fig. 3) This will indicate the end of a round.

3. Arrange the needles in a circle or triangle with the point of your first cast-on stitch in your left hand and the last cast-on stitch (and the marker) in your right hand.

4. To join in the round, insert the right needle into the first stitch on the left needle and knit the stitch, pulling the yarn tightly to eliminate any gap.

5. Continue knitting around until you reach the end of the round, indicated by the marker.

6. Slip the marker from the left to the right needle and begin knitting the new round.

7. Continue knitting to the length indicated in the pattern.

8. If you are using circular needles and the item you are knitting in the round begins to decrease, you will eventually need to change to double-pointed needles to complete the pattern. To change from a circular needle to double-pointed needles, count the number of stitches remaining on the circular needle and divide it by 3. Knit this number onto each of three double-pointed needles, using the remaining needle to knit with. (Fig. 4)

9. Continue knitting in the round on the double-pointed needles, keeping an even tension as you move from one needle to the next and slipping the marker to indicate the end of a round.

Crochet

Single Crochet

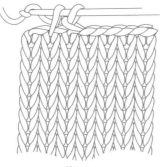

Fig. 5

This technique is used to create a decorative finish along edges, necklines, collars, and cuffs.

1. With the yarn waiting at the wrong side of the work, insert the crochet hook between two stitches from front to back and pull the yarn through to the front, creating a loop. Keeping the loop on the hook, move forward one or two rows and insert the hook into the next stitch and catch the yarn again. Pull the yarn through to the front and through the previous loop, creating a new loop on the hook. (Fig. 5) Repeat.

Chain

Fig. 6

Fig. 7

Fig. 8

1. Make a slip knot on the crochet hook.

2. Holding the hook like a pencil in your right hand and the yarn between the thumb and middle finger of your left hand, wrap the yarn up and over the hook from back to front. (Fig. 6)

3. Catch the yarn in the hook and pull it through the loop already on the hook. (Fig. 7)

4. Repeat Steps 2–3 until the chain is the desired length. (Fig. 8) Cut the yarn and pull the tail through the loop.

Finishing & Seaming

Weave in Ends

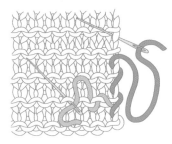

Fig. 1

Thread a loose end onto a tapestry needle and weave the yarn under and over stitches for 2"–3" along a single row on the wrong side of the knitted fabric. Cut the yarn close to the work, leaving a ½" tail. (Fig. 1)

Backstitch

Fig. 2

1 With right sides together, pin the two pieces to be seamed so the edges are even.

2 Thread a tapestry needle with approximately 18" of yarn.

3 Working from right to left, one stitch in from the edge, insert the needle under both Vs at the top of the bind-off edge and back through the first edge stitch. (Fig. 2)

4 Insert the needle through both fabrics again two stitches to the left, then back one stitch to the right.

5 Continue working back one stitch for every two stitches forward until the seaming is complete.

Kitchener Stitch

The kitchener stitch is a method for joining stitches head to head, or grafting. This method creates a stretchy seam that is almost invisible, especially when you are using a heavy yarn.

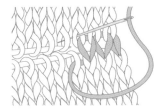

Fig. 3

1 Lay the knitted pieces that are to be joined together on your work surface with right sides up, knitting needles held parallel with the points to the right, and working stitches head to head, designating one top and one bottom. (Fig. 3)

2 Thread the tapestry needle with the working yarn. **Note:** If you left a long tail end on the piece you will begin grafting from, use it. If not, start a new yarn strand and weave in the end later.

3 Working from right to left and starting in the bottom piece, insert the tapestry needle up through the first loop as if to knit and slip the stitch off the knitting needle.

4 Insert the tapestry needle into the next loop on the bottom piece as if to purl and leave it on the knitting needle.

5 Insert the tapestry needle into the first loop on the top piece as if to purl and slip the stitch off the knitting needle.

6 Insert the tapestry needle into the next loop on the top piece as if to knit and leave it on the knitting needle.

7 Repeat Steps 3–6 until all stitches are grafted together.

8 Weave in the end along the side edge and cut it close to the work.

Mattress Stitch/Invisible Vertical Seam

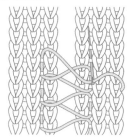

Fig. 4

1. With right sides facing up, lay the pieces edge to edge on the work surface.

2. Thread a tapestry needle with approximately 18" of yarn. At the bottom of the left piece, make one or two small stitches to anchor the yarn.

3. Leaving a 6" tail, insert the needle between the first and second stitches in the bottom corner of the right side and bring it up in the space between the first and second stitches two rows above, catching two running threads or yarn bars. Pull the yarn through in the direction of the seam, not toward you.

4. Insert the needle between the first and second stitches on the left side and bring it up again two rows above. Pull the yarn through.

5. Return to the right side. Insert the needle in the same space the yarn last came up from and bring it up two rows above, then pull the yarn through. Repeat for the left side.

6. Continue working upward from side to side, row by row, until the seaming is complete. (Fig. 4)

Blocking

Once you have completed your knitting and woven in all the loose ends, there is one more step to take before your piece is finished—blocking. Blocking helps to even out and flatten a knitted piece. You should always block individual pieces before seaming them together to make up a project.

1. To begin blocking, you will need a piece of foam board cut to 36" x 54", blocking pins, clean damp white cloths or towels, a craft knife, a straight-edge ruler, and a steam iron.

2. With craft knife and ruler, score 1" grid lines horizontally and vertically on foam board.

3. Line the knitted piece up with the grid lines and pin it to the board as indicated by the finished measurements.

4. Place damp cloths on the piece and allow to dry overnight.

5. Hold the iron above one section of the piece—without placing it directly on the knitting—and allow the steam to penetrate the fabric. Move to the next section and repeat until finished. Allow to dry again before removing the pins.

Needle Notes:
Caring for Your Needles

Knitting needles need to be clean and free of dust. If your needles get dirty, wipe them with a damp cloth and dry them thoroughly. If yarn seems to stick on them, wipe the needles, top to bottom, with heavy waxed paper. Rusted steel needles can be polished with steel wool.

Whip Stitch

Fig. 1

1. With right sides facing up, lay the pieces edge to edge on the work surface.

2. Thread a tapestry needle with approximately 18" of yarn.

3. Leaving a 6" tail, insert the needle into the first bind-off stitch on the left side from back to front. Pull the yarn through.

4. Insert the needle into the corresponding bind-off stitch on the right side from front to back and over into the next stitch on the left side from back to front. Pull the yarn through. (Fig. 1)

5. Continue working from side to side until the seaming is complete.

Running Stitch

Fig. 2

1. With right sides together, pin the two pieces to be seamed so the edges are even.

2. Thread a tapestry needle with approximately 18" of yarn.

3. Working from right to left, one stitch in from the edge, insert the needle under both Vs at the top of the bind-off edge and back through the first edge stitch.

4. Insert the needle through both fabrics again one stitch to the left, from back to front. (Fig. 2)

5. Insert the needle through both fabrics again one stitch to the left, from front to back.

6. Continue working in this manner until the seaming is complete.

Dropped Knit Stitch

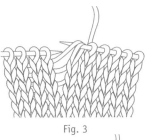

Fig. 3

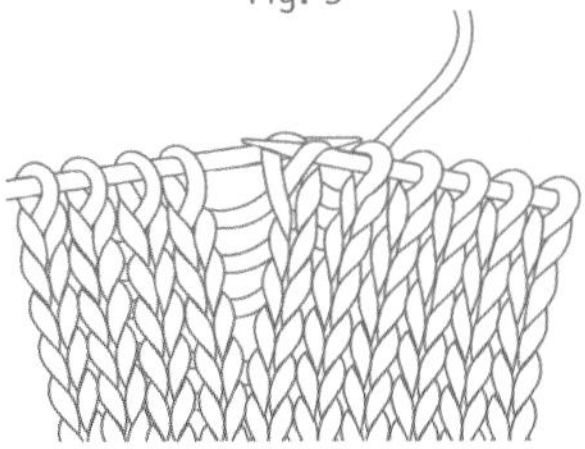

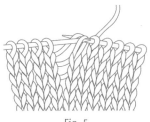

Fig. 4

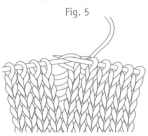

Fig. 5

Fig. 6

In the row below:

1. Insert the right needle first through the stitch below, then under the yarn of the dropped stitch. (Fig. 3)

2. Insert the left needle from back to front into the picked-up stitch and pull it up and forward. (Fig. 4)

3. Slip the lifted stitch over the yarn on the right needle and let it fall from the right needle, then from the left needle. (Fig. 5) **Note:** The dropped stitch is now restored, but facing the wrong way.

4. Insert left needle from front to back into the restored stitch, slipping it from the right to the left needle. Knit the stitch as usual. (Fig. 6)

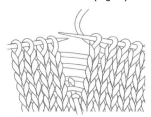

Fig. 7

Several rows below:

1. Knit to where you dropped the stitch and slip the dropped stitch onto your crochet hook. Hook the horizontal yarn, or "ladder rung," just above the dropped stitch and pull it through the dropped stitch. (Fig. 7)

2. Continue hooking ladder rungs and pulling them through until you reach the top of the ladder and can slip the stitch back on the needle.

Needle Notes:
Gently Unravel Rows

You may find that some yarns are harder than others to unravel if you've made a mistake. Keep a pair of scissors close by to snip fibers that have become entangled.

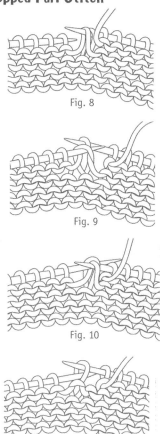

Dropped Purl Stitch

Fig. 8

Fig. 9

Fig. 10

Fig. 11

In the row below:

1. Insert the right needle from back to front first into the stitch below, then under the dropped stitch. (Fig. 8)

2. Insert the left needle into the picked-up stitch from the back and pull it upward and in front. (Fig. 9)

3. Remove the right needle tip, bringing the dropped stitch through the picked-up stitch to restore the dropped stitch to the needle. (Fig. 10)

4. Move the restored stitch from the right needle to the left, slipping the picked-up stitch off the needle. (Fig. 11) Continue work as usual.

continued on page 30

continued from page 29

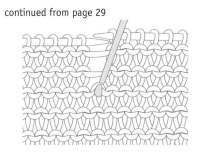

Fig. 1

Several rows below:

1. Knit to the point where you dropped the stitch and slip the dropped stitch onto your crochet hook from back to front. Draw the ladder rung just above the dropped stitch through the dropped stitch. (Fig. 1)

2. Continue working up the ladder rungs until you reach the top of the ladder and can slip the stitch back on the needle.

Dropped Stitch in Garter Stitch

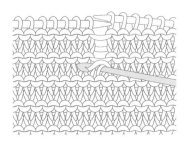

Fig. 2

1. Knit to the point where you dropped the stitch and slip the dropped stitch onto your crochet hook from the front, hooking the next ladder rung if it is on a knit row; or insert the hook from back to front into the stitch, catching the next ladder rung if it is on a purl row. (Fig. 2)

2. Continue working up the ladder rungs, matching the method to knit and purl rows until you reach the top of the ladder and can slip the stitch back on the needle.

Ripping Out Stitch By Stitch

If the mistake is on the row you are working on, rip back one stitch at a time.

1. With the knit or purl side toward you, insert the left needle from front to back into the stitch below the one on the right needle.

2. Slide the right needle out of the stitch and gently rip, or pull, the working yarn to undo the stitch.

3. Continue to rip back, stitch by stitch, to the point of the mistake.

4. Continue working the pattern as indicated.

Ripping Out Row By Row

If the mistake is located several rows below the one you are working, rip out the necessary rows.

1. Locate the row with the mistake. Mark the mistake with a safety pin.

2. Slide the knitting needle out of the stitches. Gently rip, or pull, the working yarn to undo the stitches until you are on the row above the mistake.

3. Hold your knitting with the working yarn on the right. Insert the tip of the needle into the first stitch on the row below, from back to front toward you.

4. Pull on the yarn to unravel the stitch. Make certain you have one stitch on the right needle. Continue to rip back, stitch by stitch, sliding the stitches below onto the needle until you reach the point of the mistake. Rip out the mistake.

5. Continue working the pattern as indicated.

Correcting Dropped Stitches

If you count the number of stitches on the needle and find that you have one less stitch than you should, you have probably dropped a stitch. Carefully spread out the stitches along the needle and scan the rows below the needle until the dropped stitch is located. Carefully work the tip of a safety pin into the dropped stitch, securing and stretching it out.

Felting

Felting is a process of matting and shrinking, or fulling, a project made of 100 percent wool by exposing the yarn to hot water. Soap is added to the process to help make the yarn oily and to "unlock" the wool fibers during washing. As the yarn cools and dries, the fibers tangle, or lock, into the sturdy material we recognize as felt.

The amount of shrinkage for any piece of knitting differs from yarn to yarn and is a direct result of the water temperature. Generally, you can knit a piece that is half again the size desired after felting and come close to that size when the process is complete. However, because the process is not exact, it is not very suitable for items that demand careful measurement.

It is a good idea to knit a swatch to see how your machine felts. Make a square swatch with the yarn you'll be using in your project, then toss it in your machine. Check it a number of times before the end of the cycle to get a sense of your particular machine's "felting factor."

1. To protect your washing machine from excess lint, place the item to be felted in a zippered pillow protector or mesh lingerie bag.

2. Set the machine for hot wash, longest cycle and lowest water level.

3. Add a light-colored, heavy-weight article of clothing (to create more friction) and a small amount of a mild detergent or liquid dish soap (about 2 Tbs.). **Note:** Do not use your machine's spin cycle until the last washing cycle as it takes longer to go through the whole cycle and may cause permanent creases.

4. While agitating, check on felting progress every 5 minutes. Set the machine's timer back to agitate longer if needed. Most items need 25–30 minutes of agitation, but you should still check it every few minutes.

5. When the item is felted to your liking, complete the rinse and spin cycle.

6. Remove the item immediately to prevent creasing.

7. Straighten out any corners, pull off any excess fibers, and pat lightly with towels. Allow to dry. **Note:** You may also dry the felted item in a warm dryer and steam-press the piece on a towel to form.

Needle Notes:
Faulty Felting

If your item is resisting felting or stops shrinking before you'd like it to, remove it from the washer, wring it out, and quickly plunge it into an ice water bath. Return the piece to the washer and finish felting process. If you think extra abrasion would help, toss in a couple pairs of old jeans (never use towels) with the felting project and see if that speeds the process.

Finishing Touches

Fringe

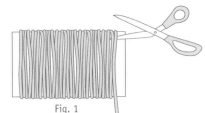

Fig. 1

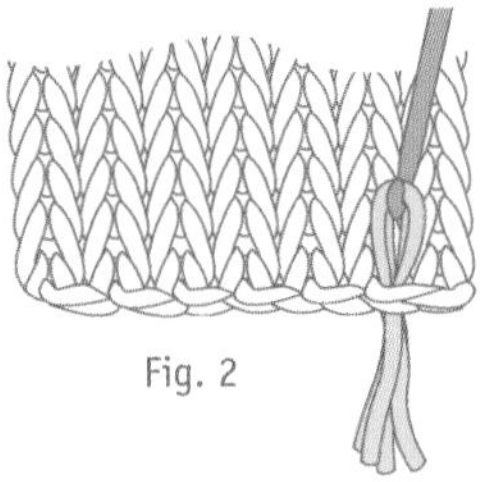

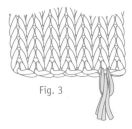

Fig. 2

Fig. 3

⑤ Repeat Steps 3–4 along the edge as desired. **Note:** It is best to begin at each end, then the middle, and work at successive halfway points for fringes that are evenly spaced.

Tassel

Fig. 4

Fig. 5

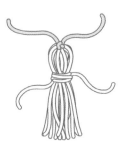

Fig. 6

① Cut a piece of cardboard to the height desired for the length of your fringe.

② Wrap yarn around the cardboard approximately 20 times and cut the yarn along one edge. Repeat as needed to get the amount of fringe you desire. (Fig. 1)

③ Insert a crochet hook through an edge stitch on your knitted piece from front to back. Fold one or more pieces of fringe yarn in half, catch the loop on the hook, and pull it through the stitch. (Fig. 2)

④ Pull the ends of the fringe yarn through the loop and cinch them so the fringe is secure. (Fig. 3)

① Cut a piece of cardboard 3"–5" wide and approximately 1" longer than the height desired for the length of your tassel.

② Wrap yarn around the cardboard until you achieve the desired fullness. (Fig. 4)

③ Thread a 12" piece of yarn onto a tapestry needle. Slip the needle under the wrapped yarn along the top edge, pull the wrapped yarn together tightly, and tie in a knot. (Fig. 5)

Note: Leave the yarn tail so you can tie the tassel onto your project.

4 Cut the wrapped yarn along the bottom edge.

5 Wrap a second 12" piece of yarn around the tassel several times, approximately 1" below the top knot and tie a knot. (Fig. 6) Thread these yarn ends onto a tapestry needle and pull down into the center of the tassel.

Pom-Pom

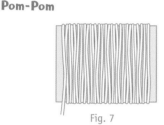

Fig. 7

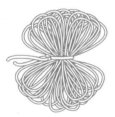

Fig. 8

Fig. 9

1 Cut a piece of cardboard as wide as the diameter desired for your pom-pom.

2 Wrap yarn around the cardboard until you achieve the desired fullness—approximately 40 times. (Fig. 7)

3 Carefully remove the yarn loops from the cardboard. Wrap an 18" piece of yarn around the center of the loops and tie in a knot. (Fig. 8) **Note:** Leave the yarn tail so you can tie the pom-pom onto your project.

4 Cut the yarn loops, fluff the pom-pom, and trim it so it is nice and round. (Fig. 9)

I-Cord

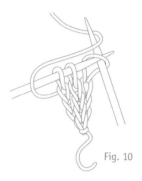

Fig. 10

This is a great method for creating a knitted rope that perfectly matches your knitted piece. It can be knitted on its own or right into a project. The I-cord is worked using two double-pointed needles.

Cast on the number of stitches indicated by the pattern—usually three to five. Without turning the needle, slide the stitches toward the right to the other end of the needle and switch that needle to the left hand. The yarn now will be coming from the stitch at the far end of the needle. Simply pull the yarn tightly across the back of the work and knit the stitches. Slide the stitches to the opposite end of the needle again, switch the needle to the left hand, and knit the stitches. Continue in this manner until the I-cord is the desired length. (After only a few rows, the work will start to look like a cord.) Bind off. (Fig. 10)

Chapter I

Scarves

✘ ✘ ✘ ✘ ✘ ✘ ✘ ✘ ✘ ✘ ✘ ✘ ✘ ✘ ✘

It used to be that if you wore a knitted scarf, it was to keep your neck warm. Now, because of the variety of yarns and pattern choices available, a scarf can also be used to add a little drama to your wardrobe. An ultra-soft scarf with an open pattern, such as our Softee Scarf, can be worn all day long in much the same way as you would wear a necklace. An extra long scarf, such as our jazzy Skelt Scarf, can be worn like a boa— barely skimming the floor—or double as a wrap-around belt.

You'll still want a scarf to tuck into your coat on cold winter days. Choose our Fuzzy Bunny Scarf or our Woven "Braid" Scarf. Our Biggy Rib Scarf offers an added benefit. It has a built-in pocket that is just the right size for stashing your cell phone or MP3 player.

All of our scarves are knit straight. Most of them can be completed in one sitting. Although they're quick and easy to complete, you'll still learn new techniques like how to alternate needle sizes for a unique garter stitch pattern, how to work the dropped wrap stitch, and how to combine a common stitch pattern with a thick/thin wicked yarn to create a whole new textured effect.

Biggy Rib Scarf

Materials
- Needles: straight, size 35 (19mm) or size to obtain gauge
- Striped sock (optional)
- Yarn: 5 balls (100g/32 yds) Rowan Biggy Print (#253 Joker)

Gauge
24 sts = 4".

Finished Size
6" x 55" (before fringe).

Instructions
- CO 12 sts.
- Continue the work,
  creating a rib stitch as follows:
  Row 1: K3, p2, k2, p2, k3.
  Row 2: P3, k2, p2, k2, p3.
- Repeat Rows 1–2 until piece
  measures 55".
- BO all sts knitwise.
- Weave in ends.
- Add fringe along short edges
  as desired.

Optional: Cut sock to form pocket.
Sew onto scarf.

Needle Notes: *Tips for Left-Handed Knitters*

The patterns in this book are written for the right-handed knitter. Most
lefties find it a bit difficult to work the stitches when they are first learning.
However, because both hands are involved in the knitting process they
soon become comfortable with the work. If you find that you cannot get the
hang of doing so much work with your right hand, simply substitute the word
"right" for "left" in the instructions and hold the diagrams up to a mirror.

Fuzzy Bunny Scarf

Materials
- Decorative elements (optional)
- Needles: straight, size 13 (9mm)
  straight, size 35 (19mm)
- Yarn: 2 balls (50g/49 yds) Berroco Monet (Madame X)
  2 balls (50g/80m) GGH Esprit (#7 Natural)

Gauge
9 sts and 8 rows = 4" in alternating garter stitch.

Finished Size
6" x 60".

Instructions
- Holding yarns together as one, CO 12 sts on size 35 needle.
- K first row with size 13 needle.
- K next row with size 35 needle.
- Continue in alternating garter stitch until piece measures 60" (or desired length).
- BO all sts knitwise.
- Weave in ends.
- Add decorative elements to each end as desired.

Needle Notes: Copy Your Pattern
Photocopy your pattern so you can make notes on it and check off your progress as you go. A copy is also easier to carry when you are on the go.

Skelt Scarf

Materials
- Needles: straight, size 11 (8mm) or size to obtain gauge
- Yarn: 2 skeins (50g/82 yds) Berroco Quest (Marron Glacé)

Gauge
13 sts and 10 rows = 4" in seed stitch.

Finished Size
4" x 80".

Instructions
- CO 13 sts.
- K in seed stitch until piece measures 80" or desired length.
- BO all sts knitwise.
- Weave in ends.

Needle Notes: *Choosing a Knitting Bag*

You will need a fabulous bag to carry all of your knitting "stuff." Look for a bag
that is large enough to hold your project, pattern, materials, and equipment.
A bag with pockets is helpful for keeping everything separated and organized.
You can choose from designer bags and funky big purses, totes and satchels,
messenger bags and backpacks, and slings and beach bags. Above all, choose
a bag that fits your own personal style. Use a cute zippered cosmetic bag
or a chic roll-up jewelry bag for carrying smaller knitting supplies.

Retro Checkered Scarf

Materials
- Lapel pins (optional)
- Needles: straight, size 10 (6mm) or size to obtain gauge
- Yarn: 2 skeins (100g/140 yds) Plymouth Fantasy Naturale (#9710)

Gauge
17 sts and 20 rows = 4" in garter stitch.

Finished Size
5½" x 65".

Instructions

- CO 25 sts.
- K 5 rows in garter stitch.
- Continue the work as follows:
  Row 1: K5, p5, k5, p5, k5
  Row 2: K5, k5, p5, k5, p5
  Row 3: K5, p5, k5, p5, k5
  Row 4: K5, k5, p5, k5, p5
  Row 5: K5, p5, k5, p5, k5
  Row 6: K5, p5, k5, p5, k5
  Row 7: K5, k5, p5, k5, p5
  Row 8: K5, p5, k5, p5, k5
  Row 9: K5, k5, p5, k5, p5
  Row 10: K5, p5, k5, p5, k5
- Repeat Rows 1–10 until piece
  measures 64".
- Work in garter stitch for five more rows.
- BO all sts knitwise.
- Weave in ends.
- Embellish with lapel pins, if desired.

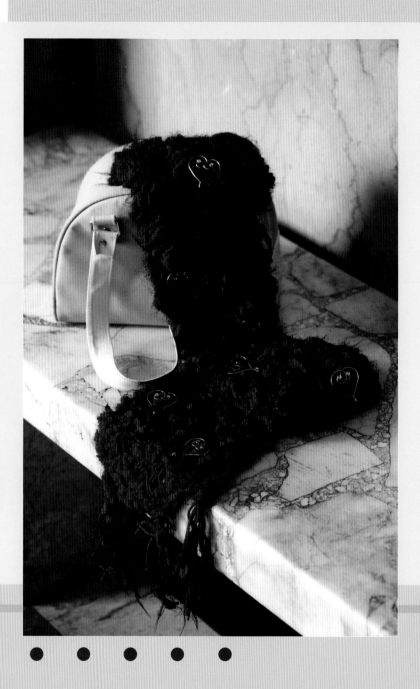

Softee Scarf

Materials
- Needles: straight, size 11 (8mm)
- Yarn: 2 balls (50g/104 yds) Berroco Softy (#2974)

Gauge
Not critical.

Finished Size
66" (before fringe).

Instructions
- CO 20 sts.
- Row 1: K all sts.
- Row 2: K all sts.
- Row 3: (RS) K8, yo twice, k1, yo 3 times, k1, yo 4 times, k1, yo 3 times, k1, yo twice, k8.
- Row 4: K1, dropping all yos.
- Row 5: K all sts.
- Row 6: K all sts.
- Row 7: K3, *yo twice, k1, yo 3 times, k1, yo 4 times, k1, yo 3 times, k1, yo twice, k6, repeat to end but k3 instead of k6.
- Row 8: Same as Row 4.
- Repeat Rows 1–8 until piece measures 66".

- BO all sts.
- Weave in ends.
- Embellish with favorite lapel pins and fringe as desired.

Woven "Braid" Scarf

Materials
- Needles: straight, size 13 (9mm)
- Yarn: 1 hank (50g/16 yds) R2 Braid (#2 Grey)
  1 ball (50g/44 yds) Anny Blatt Vega (#368 Marble)
  1 ball (100g/200 yds) Plymouth Encore Worsted (#146 White)

Gauge
No gauge.

Finished Size
5" x 48½" (before fringe).

Instructions
- Cut Braid into eight equal pieces. Cut nine lengths of Vega and 18 lengths of Encore equal to Braid pieces.
- *Tie one length of Vega and two lengths of Encore (Strand 1) onto one knitting needle, leaving enough of a tail as reserve for fringe. Tie one length of Braid (Strand 2) onto knitting needle, again allowing for fringe.* Repeat between ** until you run out of lengths (17 strands total). (Fig. 1) **Note:** The odd numbered strands should be Vega and Encore and the even numbered strands should be Braid.
- Using one strand of Vega and two strands of Encore, begin weaving back and forth through the different strands hanging from your needle. For example,

Row 1 would be over the odd strands and under the even ones, then Row 2 would be under the odd strands and over the even ones. Repeat this process until you come to the end of the lengths of yarn. (Fig. 1)
- When you come to the end of the lengths, tie Strand 1 to Strand 2, 3 to 4, and so on until Strand 9, which you tie to the strand you are actually weaving with to secure it and make sure your scarf doesn't unravel. (A square knot tends to be the best way to tie the yarn.) Once you have your working side done, work on unraveling the needle side and tying that one off too.
- Add fringe, if desired.

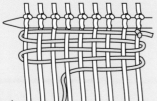

Fig. 1

Headband Scarf

Materials
- Needles: straight, size 4 (3½mm) or size to obtain gauge
- Yarn: 1 skein (127g/223 yds) TLC Amore (#3934 Plum Print)

Gauge
16 sts and 24 rows = 4".

Finished Size
3" x 25".

Instructions
- CO 1 st (this is actually the slip stitch). K as a single-stitch row for 5" to create a tie end for the headband.

Increase Section
- Row 1: Inc1, creating a 2-stitch row.
- Row 2: K all sts.
- Row 3: Inc1, inc1, creating a 4-stitch row.
- Row 4: K all sts.
- Row 5: Inc1, k2, inc1, creating a 6-stitch row.
- Row 6: K all sts.
- Row 7: Inc1, k4, inc1, creating an 8-stitch row.
- Row 8: K all sts.
- Continue in this manner, increasing until you have 16 sts across.
- K in garter stitch until your piece measures 15" in length.

Decrease Section
- Row 1: K2tog, k12, k2tog, creating 14-stitch row.
- Row 2: K across.
- Row 3: K2tog, k10, k2tog, creating 12-stitch row.
- Row 4: K across.
- Row 5: K2tog, k8, k2tog, creating 10-stitch row.
- Row 6: K across.
- Continue in this manner until you have decreased down to 1 st.
- K as single-stitch row until tie end is 5" in length.
- BO.

Great Idea! Form Meets Function
While it is fashionable, the Headband Scarf is also functional. It's a great way to keep hair dry and out of the way when washing your face.

Chapter 2

Shrugs & Ponchos

✕ ✕ ✕ ✕ ✕ ✕ ✕ ✕ ✕ ✕ ✕ ✕ ✕ ✕ ✕

When there's a chill in the air, but it's not cold enough for a sweater, you want to have a comfortable shrug or poncho. Not only can one of these short knitted jackets warm your shoulders, they can give your outfit a layered, textured look.

The actual knitting of these pieces is unbelievably easy. The poncho and shrugs are all simple rectangles. The secret is in the construction. By joining short and long edges in different ways for each of these, you create the shrug's front, back, and armholes. The Summer Shrug is one long piece that is knit beginning from the cuff of one sleeve, increasing and continuing across the back, and decreasing and ending at the cuff of the opposite sleeve—all that is left to do is seam up the sleeves.

This chapter shows you how the yarns you choose can reflect who you are and how you feel. For example, the Colinette Shrug is worked in a ribbon yarn on large needles to produce a very open, almost lacy effect and is accented with a bit of faux fur along the edges, giving it a playful and confident air.

The Summer Shrug is worked in a fine weight yarn that is variegated in a subdued palette of blues and golds, purples and pinks, and oranges. The striping effect that results reminds you of how inspired you felt sitting on a beach watching the sunset paint the horizon.

Continuous Shrug

Materials
- Needles: straight, size 10 (6mm) or size to obtain gauge
- Yarn: 2-3 balls (50g/151 yds) Rowan Kid Classic (#835)

Gauge
16 sts and 17 rows = 4" when slightly stretched.

Finished Size
XS–S (M–L).

Instructions
- CO 48 (54) sts.
- Work in k4 p4 rib until piece measures 48" (or longer for larger sizes), leaving enough yarn for BO.
- BO in rib pattern.

Finishing
- Weave in ends.
- Using mattress stitch, seam CO and BO edges together. (Fig. 1)
- Starting at this BO edge seam, measure and sew 5" on each side.

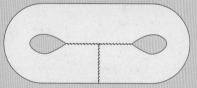

Fig. 1

Needle Notes: *Reading a Knitting Pattern*
A knitting pattern consists of instructions written out to follow the progression of the work, row by row. A pattern is usually divided into sections such as left and right, front and back, and sleeves. The key to understanding a knitting pattern is knowing what the abbreviations mean and paying attention to commas, asterisks, brackets, and parentheses.

× × × × × × × × × × × × × × × × × ×

Island Poncho

Materials
- Needles: circular, size 17 (12¾mm) or size to obtain gauge
- Ribbon: 1" satin, 60"
- Yarn: 1 hank (227g/150 yds) Ironstone Island Cotton (#27)

Gauge
Yo, p2tog [2½ times] and 4 rows = 4".

Finished Size
One size fits most.

Instructions
- CO 18 sts loosely.
- Yo, p2tog across row.
- Repeat last row until piece measures 25" when slightly stretched.
  Note: When doing a yo at the beginning of each row, make certain the yarn is feeding over the top of the right needle before purling the first 2 sts.
- Repeat for a second piece.

Finishing
- Weave in ends.
- Using mattress stitch or backstitch, seam one short end to long side of second piece, and vice versa. (Fig. 1)
- Add long fringes as desired.
- For Pareo, use length of ribbon and feed through yarn over spaces along top edge for a tie.

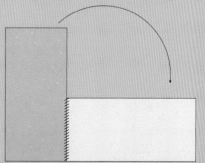

Fig. 1

Cuirass Shrug

Materials
- Needles: straight, size 35 (19mm) or size to obtain gauge
- Yarn: 1 hank (250g/137 yds) Fleece Artists Wool Slub (Burgundy)

Gauge
6 sts and 8 rows = 4".

Finished Size
XS–S.

Instructions
- CO 12 sts.
- Work in garter stitch until piece measures 56". **Note:** Knit additional inches for larger sizes.
- BO all sts.

Finishing
- Weave in ends.
- Wrap length of knitted fabric around lower back, join ends at middle of back over each shoulder, and using mattress stitch or backstitch, seam parts together in reverse T pattern. (Fig. 1)

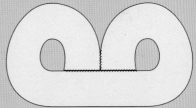

Fig. 1

Needle Notes: *Relax the Tension*

As you seam, keep tension even. Pull the yarn firmly as you go, but not so tightly that the edges will pucker. Use lengths of yarn about 18" for seaming. Longer pieces will break from the constant friction of pulling the yarn through the knitting.

Colinette Shrug

Materials
- Crochet hook: size J (6mm)
- Needles: straight, size 17 (12¾mm)
- Yarn: 2 hanks (100g/156 yds) Colinette Giotto (Raspberry)
  1 skein (50g/60 yds) Sullivans Tickle (#90247 Red)

Gauge
Not important.

Finished Size
XS–S.

Instructions
- CO 40 sts with Colinette.
- Rows 1–115: Sl1, *yo, k2tog,* repeat
  18 more times, k1.
- BO all sts.

Finishing
- Fold up corners (Fig. 1, A and B) and,
  using mattress stitch or backstitch, seam
  together, leaving opening for armholes.
  (Fig. 2)
- Using crochet hook, single crochet with
  Sullivans Tickle around all openings for
  2 rnds.

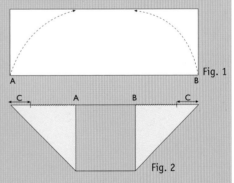

Fig. 1

Fig. 2

Needle Notes: *Correcting Too Many Stitches*

If too many stitches are on the needle, the yarn may have crossed the needle
while you were not paying attention, inadvertently increasing the number
of stitches, or the wrap may not have quite made it through the old stitch.
In the case of either of these, the stitch will need to be ripped out.

Summer Shrug

Materials
- Needles: straight, size 5 (3¾mm) or size to obtain gauge
- Yarn: 3 skeins (50g/175 yds) Koigu KPPPM (#106L)

Gauge
15 sts and 15 rows = 2".

Finished Size
45" long (each sleeve is 16½"; back is 12").

Instructions

- CO 42 sts.
- Work in K6, p6 rib across rows until piece measures 1".
- Continue in st st, increasing 2 sts, one at either end of the row every 3 rows, until you have increased to about 90 sts. **Note:** Sleeve should be 16½" long.
- Continue in st st across back for 12".
- Start decreasing 2 sts, one at either end of the row every 3 rows, until you are back down to 42 sts.
- Work in K6, p6 rib for 1".
- BO all sts.

Finishing
- Using the mattress stitch, seam each sleeve together, beginning at the ribbing and continuing for about 11½".
- Weave in ends.

Chapter 3

Belts & Caps

✖ ✖ ✖ ✖ ✖ ✖ ✖ ✖ ✖ ✖ ✖ ✖ ✖ ✖ ✖

When it comes to fashion accessories, there are two must haves: belts and hats. The right belt can complete an outfit and a spunky hat can lend a little attitude to an everyday look. This chapter combines knitting know-how with an up-to-date sense of style. These four projects are easy to make and fun to wear.

The Trendsetter Belt is knit from two furry metallic yarns held together as one to maximize the sparkle factor. This chic and elegant belt will glam up a pair of last season's jeans the instant you tie it on.

The Teen's Hat is much like you—likeable and fun to get to know. Although it is made from only one color of worsted wool, the hat features a garter stitch pattern that is accented by ridges of stockinette stitch. You can turn this hat inside out and wear it so the ridges show in reverse—pretty *and* smart.

Our second hat, the Beanie Cap, demonstrates how exciting working with color can be. Learn how to create a faux cable in your knitting while watching the subtle striping effect of a variegated yarn appear right before your eyes.

Finally, the Fall Belt teaches a lesson in fashion. It takes the simple stockinette stitch fabric, combines it with a fabulous oversized buckle, and proves that it doesn't take a lot of time or money to create something beautiful.

Trendsetter Belt

Materials
- Needles: straight, size 8 (5mm) or size to obtain gauge
- Stitch markers
- Yarn: 1 skein (50g/145 yds) Trendsetter Aura (#78 Black)
  1 skein (25g/110 yds) Trendsetter Jester (#11 Silver)

Gauge
20 sts = 4".

Finished Size
2¼" x 40" (before fringe).

Instructions
- Holding both yarns together as one, CO 10 sts.
- Work in garter stitch until desired length.

Finishing
- Weave in ends.
- Make fringe with both yarns together.
- Attach fringe as desired along short edges.

Great Idea! Jot Down the Details
Keep a notebook with a page or two dedicated to each project you knit. Include a photocopy of the pattern, the yarn label, and a sample of the yarn you used, needle size and gauge information, the size and dimensions of the project, how much it cost to knit the item, notes about problems you had or changes you made, the start and finish dates, and a picture of the project when it is finished. This way you can always recreate a project or share the pattern with a friend.

Teen's Hat

Materials

- Needles: 16" circular, size 9 (5½mm) or size to obtain gauge
  double-pointed, size 9 (5½mm)
  tapestry
- Stitch markers
- Yarn: 1 skein (50g/110 yds) Knit Picks Wool of the Andes (Avocado) for CC
  1 skein (50g/110 yds) Knit Picks Wool of the Andes (Grass) for MC

Gauge

22 sts and 28 rows = 1".

Finished Size

Completed hat will fit head circumference of 20"–22".

Instructions

Note: Change from circular needle to double-pointed needles when there becomes too few sts to complete rnds on the circular needle.

- CO 80 sts with MC on circular needle, leaving a 12" tail.
- Join in the rnd, placing marker for the beginning of the rnd.
- Rnd 1: *P10, place marker*, repeat * * around all 80 sts.
- Rnds 2–8: P.
- Rnds 9–11: K.
- Rnds 12–24: P.
- Rnd 25: *P2tog, p3, p2tog*, repeat * * around all 80 sts. (8 sts left between markers)
- Rnds 26–28: K.
- Rnds 29–34: P.
- Rnd 35: *P3, p2tog, p3*, repeat * * around all 64 sts. (7 sts left between markers)
- Rnds 36–38: K.
- Rnds 39–41: P.
- Rnds 42–44: K.
- Rnd 45: *P5, p2tog*, repeat * * around all 56 sts. (6 sts left between markers)
- Rnds 46–47: P.
- Rnd 48: *P2, p2tog, p2*, repeat * * around all 48 sts. (5 sts left between markers)
- Rnds 49–50: P.

Needle Notes: *Using Circular Needles*

Circular needles come in a variety of tips, but nearly all of them have plastic joining wires. If these wires are too curled, simply put them in hot water to straighten them.

- Rnd 51: *P2tog, p3*, repeat * * around all 40 sts. (4 sts left between markers)
- Rnds 52–53: P.
- Rnd 54: *P1, p2tog, p1*, repeat * * around all 32 sts. (3 sts left between markers)
- Rnds 55–56: P.
- Rnd 57: *P1, p2tog*, repeat * * around all 24 sts. (2 sts left between markers)

Finishing

- Cut yarn, leaving a 10" tail. Thread the tail onto a tapestry needle, pull it through remaining sts twice, tighten and weave in the end.

- Instead of weaving in CO tail, thread it onto the tapestry needle and loosely stitch up side of hat for 4½", and then stitch back down again. Pull tightly to create gathered edge. Secure the gather by weaving in the leftover end.

Make Bow

Knit a 10" I-cord with CC on double-pointed needles. Create two loops and secure by tying a 12" piece of yarn tightly around the center of the bow, and knot it. Use remaining yarn to sew it in place over the gather.

Needle Notes: Using Different Needles

Experiment by knitting with various types of needles. You may find that you prefer wood or bamboo needles to better control your knitting, or that you like to speed it up with nickel or aluminum. Use the needle type you find most comfortable. Similarly, you may favor straight needles over circular needles; remember, though, that if you use straight needles for a circular project, you'll need to sew together the edges into a seam.

Beanie Cap

Materials
- Needles: 16" circular, size 8 (5mm) or size to obtain gauge
  double-pointed, size 8 (5mm)
- Yarn: 1 ball (50g/92 yds) Filatura Di Crosa Print 127 (#34)

Gauge
18 sts and 20 rows = 4" measured over pattern stitch.

Finished Size
Youth/Ladies.

Instructions
Note: Change from circular needle to double-pointed needles when there becomes too few sts to complete rnds on the circular needle.

Faux Cable Stitch
K into second stitch on left needle but leave on needle, k into first stitch on needle then take both sts off needle.

- CO 70 sts on circular needle.
- Join sts in the round.
- Work k1 p1 rib for 4 rows.

Pattern
- *P5, faux cable stitch, p1, faux cable stitch* across row.
- Repeat this row until 6½" from CO edge.

Crown Shaping
- K8, k2tog across row. (63 sts)
- K1 rnd.
- K7, k2tog across row. (56 sts)
- K1 rnd.
- K6, k2tog across row. (49 sts)
- K1 rnd.
- K5, k2tog across row. (42 sts)
- K1 rnd.
- K4, k2tog across row. (35 sts)
- K1 rnd.
- K3, k2tog across row. (28 sts)
- K1 rnd.
- K2, k2tog across row. (21 sts)
- K1 rnd.
- K1, k2tog across row. (14 sts)
- K1 rnd.
- K2tog across row. (7 sts)
- Pull yarn through remaining sts and secure.

Fall Belt

Materials
- Circular wooden belt buckle
- Needles: straight, size 11 (8mm) or size to obtain gauge
  tapestry
- Yarn: ½ skein (100g/66 yds) Rowan Ribbon Twist (#122 Regency)

Gauge
12 sts and 12 rows = 4".

Finished Size
2" x 48".

Instructions
- CO 6 sts.
- Work in st st for 48".
- BO all sts.

Finishing
- Weave in ends.
- Thread a tapestry needle with a 12"
  piece of yarn. Fold one short end of
  knitting over belt buckle and sew down,
  using the whipstitch.
- Iron knitting flat.

Needle Notes: *Check Your Work*

As you are knitting, it may be helpful to periodically check your work by counting the stitches after each row. One stitch more or less than you cast on (unless you have been working increases or decreases) means that something is wrong in the last row worked.

Chapter 4

Warmies

✖ ✖ ✖ ✖ ✖ ✖ ✖ ✖ ✖ ✖ ✖ ✖ ✖ ✖ ✖

After working the patterns in this chapter, you should be a pro at knitting in the round and creating a rib stitch pattern. This stretchy fabric is just right for knitted pieces that you want to hug your body.

Our cute Tube Top/Skirt is so versatile. As its name implies, it can be worn as a top or as a skirt—next to your skin or layered over a T-shirt and jeans. Its wide stripes help accentuate the curves you never knew you had.

For your hands, fingerless gloves are the ultimate when it comes to form meeting function. This chapter gives you three different lengths to choose from.

You can pair our full-length Arm Warmers with your favorite halter top to give it a touch of class. These removable sleeves might also be the perfect practical gift for a friend who plays a cold weather outdoor sport such as soccer—she can wear them while she is waiting to play and quickly slip them off when the coach calls her name.

You can't forget your feet when you're talking about staying warm. A pair of striped Slippers with a drawstring opening will keep your tootsies nice and toasty on those chilly winter days. Ours are hot pink and black, but you can knit them in your school colors or to match your favorite pair of pajamas.

Slippers

Materials

- Black thread and sewing needle
- Elbow patches (to cut and use as soles): black suede, 2
- Needles: double-pointed, size 9 (5½mm) or size to obtain gauge
- Stitch markers
- Yarn: 1 skein (113g/ 190 yds) Brown Sheep Lamb's Pride Worsted (Black) for MC
  1 skein (113g/ 190 yds) Brown Sheep Lamb's Pride Worsted (Fuchsia) for CC
  1 yd scrap of cotton (bright color)

Gauge

20 sts and 28 rows = 4".

Finished Size

Small/6–8 shoe size
(Large/8½–10 shoe size).

Instructions

Cuff

- CO 40 (48) sts with MC.
- Divide sts among three needles: 20 (24) sts on Needle One, 10 (12) sts on Needle Two, and 10 (12) sts on Needle Three.
- Join in the round, placing marker for beginning of rnd.
- Work 6 rnds in k2 p2 rib.
- Change to CC and work 4 rnds in st st.
- Dropping all other yarns at the back of piece, k across 20 (24) sts on first needle with scrap yarn.

Gusset

- Go back to beginning of rnd and reknit all 20 (24) sts with MC, complete rnd with MC.

- K3 more rnds with MC.
- K4 rnds with CC.
- K4 rnds MC.
- Repeat last eight rnds 3 (4) times.

Toe

- Change to CC.
- Rnd 1: Needle One—K1, k2tog, k until there are 3 sts left on needle, ssk, k1.
- Needle Two—K1, k2tog, k remaining sts on needle.

77

- Needle Three—K until there are 3 sts left on needle, ssk, k1.
- Rnd 2: K all sts.
- Repeat these two rnds, continuing stripe pattern (4 rnds CC, 4 rnds MC), until there are only 20 (24) sts left.
- When there are only 20 (24) sts left, move sts from Needle Three onto Needle Two so there are 10 (12) sts on Needle One and 10 (12) sts on Needle Two.
- Use kitchener stitch to close.

Afterthought Heel
- Carefully remove scrap yarn while placing sts onto two needles.
  There should be 20 (24) sts on each needle, or 40 (48) sts total.
- Divide sts on needle closest to toe onto two needles, 10 (12) sts each.
- Starting at needle with 20 (24) sts (Needle One), k across all 20 (24) sts, then pick up 1 st in space between Needles One and Two.
- K across all sts on Needles Two and Three, and pick up 1 st between Needles One and Three. There will be 42 (50) sts total.
- Rnd 1: Needle One—K1, k2tog, k until there are 3 sts left on the needle, ssk, k1.
- Needle Two—K1, k2tog, k remaining sts on needle.
- Needle Three—K until there are 3 sts left on needle, ssk, k1.
- Rnd 2: K all sts.
- Repeat these two rnds until there are only 18 (22) sts left. When there are only 18 (22) sts left, move sts from Needle Three onto Needle Two so there are 9 (11) sts on Needle One and 9 (11) sts on Needle Two.
- Use kitchener stitch to close.

Finishing
- Weave in all ends.
- Cut one 2" circle and one 3½" circle out of one suede elbow patch. Using sewing needle and thread, whipstitch 2" circle to heel and 3½" circle to toe.
- Make a second slipper!

Great Idea! Reinforcing the Soles
While we used an elbow patch on the slippers to extend the wear, you could also use heavy suede on the soles. You may need to use a leather punch to make holes in the suede so that it's easier to sew them to the bottom of the slippers.

Wrist Warmers

Materials
- Needles: 5 double-pointed, size 3 (3¼mm)
- Stitch markers
- Yarn: 1 hank (50g, 175 yds) Koigu KPPPM (#P432)

Gauge
24 sts = 4" in K2 p2 rib when stretched.

Finished Size
One size fits all.

Instructions
Note: Gauge is not too important for this project as the k2 p2 rib is very stretchy and forgiving—just make sure it's not too loose!
- CO 44 sts.
- Divide sts evenly among four needles and join in the round.
- Work in k2 p2 rib until piece measures 5".

Shape Thumb Gusset
- Next Rnd: Work 23 sts in k2 p2 rib, place marker, work to end of rnd in k2 p2 rib.
- Next Rnd: *K2, p2* 5 times, k2, kfb, slip marker, kfb, *k2, p2* 5 times.
- Next Rnd: *K2, p2* 5 times, k2, p4, *k2, p2* 5 times.
- Next Rnd: *K2, p2* 5 times, k2, p1, kfb, slip marker, kfb, p1, *k2, p2* 5 times.
- Next Rnd: *K2, p2* 5 times, k2, p6, *k2, p2* 5 times.
- Next Rnd: *K2, p2* 5 times, k2, p2, kfb, slip marker, kfb, p2, *k2, p2* 5 times.
- Next Rnd: *K2, p2* to end of rnd. There are now 48 sts.
- Remove marker on next rnd. Continue working in k2 p2 rib without increase until piece measures 7".

Thumbhole
- *K2, p2* 4 times. BO 10 sts in ribbing. P2, *k2, p2* 5 times.
- Next Rnd: *K2, p2* 4 times. Turn work so inside of wrist warmer is facing you. Using the knit-on cast on method, CO 11 sts. Turn work so outside is facing you again. Sl 1 st, and pass 11th CO st over slipped st and off needle. (This joins the corner of the thumbhole and prevents a gap between sts.)
- P1, *k2, p2* 5 times.

Palm
- Continue working in k2 p2 rib to 2" above thumbhole. The entire piece should now measure 9" from beginning.
- BO all sts in rib pattern.

Finishing
- Weave in all ends.
- Make a second wrist warmer!

× × × × × × × × × × × × × × × × ×

Tube Top/Skirt

Materials
- Needles: 29" circular, size 8 (5mm) or size to obtain gauge
- Yarn: 1 ball (50g/86 yds) Debbie Bliss Merino Aran (#505)
  1 ball (50g/86 yds) Debbie Bliss Merino Aran (#508)
  1 ball (50g/86 yds) Debbie Bliss Merino Aran (#602)
  1 ball (50g/86 yds) Debbie Bliss Merino Aran (#703)

Gauge
32 sts and 26 rows = 4" in k2 p2 rib.

Finished Size
9½" x 15½".

Instructions
- CO 141 sts.
- Join sts in the round.
- Work in k2 p2 rib all around, knitting last stitch with first and continuing in k2 p2 rib for the entire piece, changing colors as you finish each skein. When your piece measures approximately 13½", you can add interest by knitting straight for the last 2", creating a little slit that can be worn in the back or the front.
- BO all sts.

Finishing
- Weave in all ends.

Arm Warmers

Materials
- Needles: 8½" circular, size 6 (4mm) or size to obtain gauge
- Stitch markers
- Yarn: 3 skeins (50g/99 yds) GHH Capri (#13)

Gauge
22 sts and 28 rows = 4".

Finished Size
16" long.

Instructions
- CO 53 sts.
- Join sts in the round.
- Work in k2 p2 rib all around, knitting last stitch with first and continuing in k2 p2 rib for 2".
- K for 5" (sts should look like st st).
- For next 6", decrease 1 st by k2tog every 3 rnds. Place a stitch marker at first decrease so your decreases are all consistent. This should leave you with 40 sts.
- Work in k2 p2 rib for 4 rnds.
- Continuing in k2 p2 rib, knit straight (not in the round) for 6 rows, creating a button hole the size of your thumb.
- Continuing with k2 p2 rib, work in the round for 5 more rnds.
- BO all sts.

Finishing
- Weave in all ends.
- Make a second arm warmer!
- You can embellish the cuffs of arm warmers with lace or other trims for a personal style.

Needle Notes: *Allow for Stretch*
When adding ribbon or trim to the edge of a knitting project,
be sure to allow for stretch. It's best to weave the trim into the ribbing.

× × × × × × × × × × × × × × ×
Hand Warmers

Materials
- Needles: 5 double-pointed, size 8 (5mm) or size to obtain gauge
- Yarn: 1 skein (50g/55 yds) Noro Lotus (#155)

Gauge
16 sts and 25 rows = 4" in st st.

Finished Size
4" x 4½".

Instructions
- CO 32 sts.
- Divide sts evenly among four needles and join in the round.
- Rnds 1–4: *K1, p1, repeat from * to end of rnd.
- Rnds 5–11: K.
- Rnd 12 (thumbhole round): K to last 4 sts on Needle Four. BO 4 sts.
- Rnd 13: K to end of Needle Four. CO 4 sts on Needle Four.
- Rnds 14–24: K.
- Rnds 25–28: *K1, p1, repeat from * to end of rnd.
- BO all sts.

Finishing
- Weave in all ends.
- Make a second hand warmer.

Needle Notes: *Identifying Resilient Yarns*
Different types of yarns have different qualities of resiliency,
or ability to bounce back. Wool is the queen of yarns for its ability
to keep its shape, while cotton is less resilient and more likely
to stretch. Ribbon yarn, used by itself, is the least resilient.

Chapter 5

Purses & Handbags

✕ ✕ ✕ ✕ ✕ ✕ ✕ ✕ ✕ ✕ ✕ ✕ ✕ ✕

Everyone needs a handbag or two for stashing and carrying her stuff. You'll want to knit a small to medium-sized purse for holding everyday items such as your cell phone, lunch money, keys, and lipstick. Try our Recycled Yarn Bag—a simply shaped envelope with garter stitch detailing and a long shoulder strap; our cool stripy Bag with Pom-Poms—a slightly larger bag with two short braided handles; or our Felted Purse with Handles—a sturdy, open box-shaped purse to which we added two plastic handles.

You'll also need a large tote for carrying schoolbooks, dance gear, or even your knitting project and supplies. All of our big purses are knit oversized in bulky-weight 100-percent wool and are felted to make them stronger and more durable. Some of our totes, such as the Felted Tigress Bag with its free-form design and bold combination of colors, will appeal to your wild side, while others, like the Felted Purse with its uniform striping pattern and harmonious color scheme, will speak directly to the serious-minded sophisticate in you.

Once you have selected a small purse and a large bag for everyday activities, you may want to spoil yourself with a special evening-style bag, too—there are four to choose from in this chapter. Each of these can be adjusted to color coordinate with any outfit you might choose for a night out on the town.

Felted Purse

Materials

- Needles: circular, size 10½ or 11
  double-pointed, size 10½ or 11
- Yarn: 2 balls (50g/110 yds) Noro Kureyon wool (#95)
  3 balls (113g/190 yds) Brown Sheep Lamb's Pride (#M28 Chianti)

Gauge

Not important.

Finished Size

13" x 10" x 6".

Instructions

- With Brown Sheep, CO 160 sts
  on circular needle.
- Join in the round and knit for 10".
- Change to Noro and knit stripes,
  changing yarns as desired until two balls
  of Noro and two balls of Brown Sheep
  are knit up. **Note:** Save a few yards for
  binding off and seaming.
- BO all sts.

Finishing

- Using mattress stitch or backstitch, seam
  bottom edges.
- With wrong side
  out and seam flat
  and centered
  across bottom,
  pull out corners
  at base and back-
  stitch 4½" from
  tip of triangle
  edges. (Fig. 1) This should yield 9" seam
  from side to side.
- Weave in all ends.

Fig. 1

I-cord

- With remaining ball of Brown Sheep,
  CO 4 sts on one double-pointed needle
  and k.
- Push sts to opposite end of needle
  and k again.
- Continue in this manner until I-cord
  measures 72".
- Felt I-cord and purse.
- To thread I-cord
  through purse,
  cut eight ½"
  slits with sharp
  scissors 1¼" down from top of purse and
  centered approximately 8" apart on front
  and back and 2" apart on shorter sides.
  (Fig. 2)

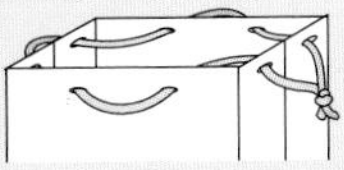

Fig. 2

Optional: Add beaded trim or embellishments of your choice to front of felted
purse.

Felted Tigress Bag

Materials
- Button
- Needles: circular, size 15 (10mm)
- Scrap embroidery floss of matching color
- Stitch markers
- Suede handles: 12"
- Yarn: 2 hanks (200g/181 yds) Classic Elite Tigress (#7052 Tigger)

Gauge
10 sts = 4".

Finished Size
15" x 9" x 5".

Instructions
Bottom of Bag
- CO 35 sts.
- K in st st for 15 rows.

Body of Bag
- Pick up 100 sts along edge of bottom.
- Join first and last CO sts.
- K in st st for approximately 12"–14".
- BO all sts.

Finishing
- Weave in all ends.
- Felt bag.
- Adjust handles to desired position, and then sew through perforations with embroidery floss.
- Add buttonhole and button between handles on each side.

Felted Mini Purse

Materials
- Needles: 16" circular, size 10¾ (7mm)
- Stitch markers
- Trim (optional)
- Yarn: 80 yds heavy-worsted weight 100% wool (red)

Gauge
14 sts = 4" (after felting).

Finished Size
6" x 8½".

Instructions
- Using very loose CO, CO 42 sts.
- K1 row.
- Place marker and join sts in the round.
- K in st st for 2".

Shape Handles
- Next Rnd: K6 sts, BO 8 sts, k12 sts, BO 8 sts, k6 sts.
- Next Rnd: K6 sts, turn work and CO 8 sts using knit-on cast on method, turn and k12 sts, turn work and CO 8 sts, turn work and k6 sts.
- Continue working in st st until approximately 2 yards of yarn remains.
- BO all sts.

Finishing
- Weave in all ends.
- Lay purse flat so handles line up and sew BO edge shut using whipstitch or mattress stitch. **Note:** Be careful not to pull too tightly on sewing yarn as bottom edge will pucker.
- Felt purse.

Great Idea! *Adding Embellishments*

Embellishing is a great way to take a simple project and make it unique. You don't have to go far to find fabulous trim or a collection of buttons that will add a bit of glitz to your knitting. Look at your local craft or discount store for bracelets, necklaces, beads, silk flowers, ribbons, lace, trims, charms, and more. Don't forget to check out antiques shops and second-hand shops, too. Once you have found the perfect piece, simply pin it or stitch it in place as desired.

Felted Purse with Handles

Materials
- Needles: 24" circular, size 13 (9mm)
  tapestry
- Plastic handles: 2
- Stitch markers
- Yarn: 1 skein (100g/132 yds) Cascade Pastaza (#84)
  1 skein (100g/132 yds) Cascade Pastaza (#85)

Gauge
Not important.

Finished Size
13" x 6" x 3".

Instructions
- CO 80 sts with dark color.
- Place marker and join in the round.
- K in st st until piece measures 5".
- Drop dark color and change to
  light color.
- K in st st for 4 rnds.
- Drop light color and change
  to dark color.
- K in st st for 5".
- Drop dark color and change
  to light color.
- K in st st for 4 rounds.
- Drop light color and change
  to dark color.
- K in st st for 5".
- Drop dark color and change
  to light color.
- K in st st for 4 rounds.
- Drop light color and change
  to dark color.
- K in st st for 4".
- BO all sts.

Finishing
- Thread a tapestry needle with dark color.
- Fold BO edge over 2" and sew,
  using whipstitch.
- Sew bottom seam together, using
  mattress stitch or backstitch.
- With wrong side out and seam flat and
  centered across bottom, pull out corners
  at base and back-
  stitch 2" from tip
  of triangle edges.
  (Fig. 1)
- Weave in all ends.
- Felt purse.
- After desired felt-
  ing has occurred
  and purse is dry,

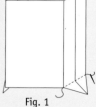

Fig. 1

thread a tapestry needle with dark color
yarn. Sew plastic handles onto each
side, making certain they are even.

Bag with Pom-Poms

Materials
- Crochet hook: size I
- Needles: straight, size 9 (5½mm) or size to obtain gauge
- Yarn: 1 skein (100g/135 yds) Manos del Uruguay (#05) for MC
  1 skein (100g/135 yds) Manos del Uruguay (#I)
  1 skein (100g/135 yds) Manos del Uruguay (#68)
  1 skein (100g/135 yds) Manos del Uruguay (#53)

Gauge
18 sts and 24 rows = 4" in st st.

Finished Size
13" x 14".

Instructions

Back
- CO 45 sts in MC.
- Work in st st as follows:
  Row 1: K, increasing 1 st at each end.
  Row 2: P.
  Repeat Rows 1–2 four more times.
  (55 sts)
- Continue in st st until bag measures 10", ending with p row.
- Decrease 1 st at each end every k row five times. (45 sts)
- Continue in st st until bag measures 14½".
- BO all sts.
- Weave in ends.

Front
- Work as for back, changing colors to form stripes as desired.

Pom-Poms
- Make one 3" pom-pom out of color #68.
- Make one 4" pom-pom out of colors #05 and #53 together.

Handles
- Cut six strands of each color 48" long.
- Place strands together and make a knot 6" from one end. Braid length until 6" remain. Knot remaining end.
- Make a second handle.

Assembly
- Using crochet hook and MC and with wrong sides facing, single crochet from top decrease around back to decrease on opposite side.
- Attach handles to right side of front and back by sewing knots onto purse.
- Attach pom-poms to strap by tying them on.

Evening Bag

Materials

- Needles: straight, size 3 (3¼mm) or size to obtain gauge
- Stitch holders: 2
- Yarn: 1 skein (50g/198 yds) S. Charles Ritratto (#77)

Gauge

24 sts and 18 rows = 4".

Finished Size

7" x 6 ½".

Instructions

- CO 50 sts.
- Work in st st for 1".
- K15 sts, BO 20 sts, k remaining 15 sts.
- Slide one set of 15 sts onto stitch holder.
- Work second set of 15 sts in st st for 1".
- Cut yarn, leaving a tail, and slide onto stitch holder.
- Pick up first set of 15 sts from stitch holder and work in st st for 1".
- CO 20 sts using knit-on cast on method.
- Pick up second set of 15 sts from holder and continue in st st for 3".
- Repeat previous pattern of k15, BO 20, k15.
- Once you have created a second opening, work in st st for another 8".
- Repeat k15, BO 20, k15 pattern one last time to create a third opening.
- Work in st st for 1".
- BO all sts.

Finishing

- Iron purse flat with steam, taking care to not stretch the fabric. Fold so openings line up to create a handle.
- Seam side edges using the mattress stitch.
- Weave in ends.

Clutch Purse

Materials

- Crochet hook: size I
- Fabric: 9" x 7" piece for lining
- Needles: straight, size 8 (5mm) or size to obtain gauge
- Sewing machine (optional)
- Sewing needle and thread
- Yarn: 2 balls (50g/99 yds) Muench String of Pearls (#4001)
- Zipper: 7"

Gauge

14 sts and 13 rows = 4".

Finished Size

8" x 4½".

Instructions

Clutch

- Holding two strands together, CO 31 sts.
- Row 1: K1, *p1, k1*, repeat * * to end of row.
- Row 2: Repeat Row 1. **Note:** These two rows form seed stitch pattern.
- Repeat Rows 1–2 until piece measures 9".
- BO all sts.

Finishing

- Fold rectangle in half from top to bottom, weaving in ends and using mattress stitch to seam sides.

Handle

- Still holding two strands together and using crochet hook, chain for 9" (or however long you need to create a loop to fit around your wrist), turn, single crochet to end, and pull tail through last loop.
- Attach both ends of loop handle to one side of purse and weave in ends.

Lining

- Fold fabric rectangle in half with right sides together so it is 4½" x 7"; iron.
- Fold out ½" from top on each side and iron them down.
- Using a sewing machine or by hand, sew zipper to lining about ¼" from zipper's teeth. **Note:** The right side of the lining should always be on the inside.
- After you sew in the zipper, sew up the sides on the lining.
- Once you have the lining completely sewn together, unzip the zipper and insert the lining into the purse. By hand, sew the zipper to the purse around the top edge.

Recycled Yarn Bag

Materials
- Button: 1"
- Crochet hook: size J
- Needles: 24" circular, size 11 (8mm) or size to obtain gauge
  double-pointed, size 8 (5mm)
- Sewing needle and thread
- Yarn: 110 yds. recycled super-chunky weight

Gauge
10½ sts = 4".

Finished Size
6¾" x 7¼".

Instructions

Make Bag
- CO 20 sts on circular needle.
- Work in st st for 66 rows,
  ending with RS facing for next row.
- Work in rev st st for 4 rows.
- Work in st st for 4 rows.
- Work in rev st st for 4 rows.
- BO all sts.

Finishing
- Fold CO edge up to 10 rows below first
  set of rev st st. **Note:** This will make up the
  body of the bag, with st st being on outside. The extra rows will make the flap.
- Turn inside out and, using mattress
  stitch, sew the side seams.
- Weave in ends.
- Turn right side out.

Button Loop
- Using crochet hook, chain 15 sts (or
  long enough to fit over your button).
- Sew one end of chain onto center of flap
  and make loop. Sew opposite end of
  chain onto flap, just next to previously
  sewn end.
- Fold flap over top of front of bag.
  Sew button onto front of bag so it lines
  up with button loop.

Strap
- CO 4 sts on one double-pointed needle
  and k.
- Push sts to opposite end of needle
  and k again.
- Continue in this manner until I-cord
  measures 47" (or desired length).
- Sew each end of I-cord into bag so
  seams blend into each other.

Karaoke Felted Purse

Materials
- Button: 1½"
- Needles: double-pointed, size 10½ (6½mm)
  straight, size 10½ (6½mm)
- Sewing needle and thread
- Yarn: 5 balls (50g/110 yds) Karaoke (#285 Intensity)

Gauge
Not important.

Finished Size
19" x 17½" (before felting).
13" x 12½" (after felting).

Instructions

Purse Front
- CO 60 sts.
- Work in st st, decreasing 1 st at
  the beginning of k rows, every 8 rows,
  six times.
- Work 6 rows without decreasing.
- Increase in second st of next row.
- Continue to increase 1 st on k rows,
  every 8 rows, five more times.
- Work 6 rows without increasing.

Purse Back
- P next row (this makes a ridge)
  on RS of your work.
- Work 5 rows in st st.
- Decrease 1 st at beginning of
  next row (knit row).
- Decrease 1 st every 8 rows,
  five more times.
- Work 6 rows without decreasing.
- Increase in second st of next knit row,
  every 8 rows, six times.
- Work 4 rows without increases.

Note: These increases and decreases cause the purse to be curved at the top. Because you are doing them only on the knit rows, the top will be curved and the bottom will be straight.
- BO all sts loosely.

Attached I-cord Edging
- Working on WS and using double-pointed needle, CO 3 sts.
- *Slide sts to other end of needle. With second double-pointed needle, k2 sts. Sl last st knitwise to right needle, and pick up st from body of purse. K these 2 sts tog.*
- Repeat from * until complete top of purse is edged.
- BO all sts.

Purse Bottom
- CO 3 sts.
- K all rows, increasing 1 st at beginning of next 9 rows. (12 sts)

- Work even until piece measures 16½".
- K1, k2tog at beginning of each row until 3 sts remain.
- BO sts.

Button Loop
- At center of purse front, pick up 4 sts and k all rows until loop measures 6".
- BO sts.
- Sew unattached end to purse to form loop.

Strap
- Pick up 5 sts at one side of purse.
- Work a 5 st I-cord for 24".
- Sew live sts at other side of purse.

Finishing
- Weave in all ends.
- Using mattress stitch or backstitch, sew bottom onto body of the purse.
- Felt bag.
- Sew button onto purse front.

Needle Notes: *Defining Yarn Fibers*

Yarns can be found in both natural fibers such as wool, cotton, silk, rayon, angora, cashmere, and mohair, and in synthetic (man-made) fibers such as polyester, acrylic, and nylon. The type of fiber or fibers used to make up the yarn is also referred to as its "content."

Sparkling Purse

Materials
- Crochet hook: size G (4mm)
- Decorative button
- Gold-plated chain or beaded trim: 42"
- Needles: straight, size 6 (4mm) or size to obtain gauge
- Sewing needle and thread
- Yarn: 1 skein (50g/205 yds) Ironstone Paris Nights (#23) for yarn A
  1 skein (25g/85 yds) Filatura di Crosa Aton (#901 Gold) for yarn B
  1 skein (50g/60 yds) Sullivans Tickle (Retro Pink) for yarn C
  1 skein (20g/77 yds) Trendsetter Shadow (#22) for yarn D

Gauge
16 sts = 4".

Finished Size
5½" x 6".

Instructions
- Holding one strand of yarn A and one strand of yarn B together, CO 25 sts.
- Work in st st for 30 rows.
- Change to one strand of yarn C and one strand of yarn D held together.
- Work in st st for 20 rows.
- Change back to yarns A and B.
- Work 30 rows in st st.
- BO all sts.

Finishing
- Weave in ends.
- Fold in half and, using mattress stitch, seam sides together.
- With one strand of yarn B and crochet hook, single crochet around top of purse.
- Center and attach button onto top front of purse.
- With one strand of yarn B and crochet hook, chain 16 sts.
- Center and attach both ends of yarn chain onto top back of purse to create a loop for the button closure.
- Using sewing needle and thread, sew gold chain or beaded trim onto both sides of purse for a handle.

Great Idea! Lining Your Handbag
If you find that your treasures are slipping through the knitting, line the bag with a complementary colored fabric. Make a rectangle, fold it in half, sew the side seams, and insert as a liner into the bag. Sew in top edges for security.

Chapter 6

Accessories

❌ ❌ ❌ ❌ ❌ ❌ ❌ ❌ ❌ ❌ ❌ ❌ ❌ ❌ ❌

Did you know you could knit cover-ups for some of the things you use most? Forget about buying a protective jacket for your MP3 player—you can knit one yourself and choose your own colors. Our I-Pod Cozy is so chic, all your friends will want one, too.

Personalize the H_2O you carry to soccer practice by slipping it into one of our handled water bottle holders. Choose an open pattern fabric that allows you to keep an eye on your water level or a thick and bumpy garter stitch fabric that will help your beverage stay cooler longer.

Don't overlook all those throw pillows in your bedroom. Create visual interest in your interior decorating by covering one or two of them. Our Fuzzy Pillow pattern takes the stockinette stitch to design school by combining it with a feathery-soft multicolored yarn to create a slipcover that is so irresistibly cuddly, it may give your favorite teddy bear a little competition.

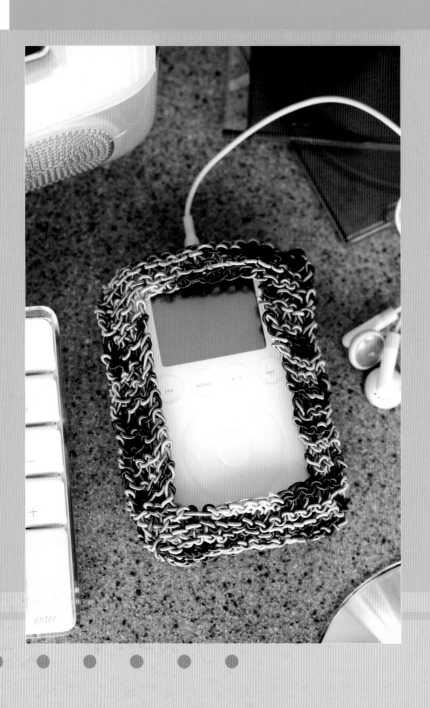

I-Pod Cozy

Materials
- Needles: straight, size 7 or size to obtain gauge
- Yarn: 1 hank (50g/55 yds) Noro Daria (#6)

Gauge
17 sts and 33 rows = 4" in garter stitch.

Finished Size
3½" x 4½".

Instructions
Note: When winding the yarn, make two balls.

Front
- With one ball, CO 16 sts.
- Work in garter stitch for 5 rows.
- Row 6: K4, BO 8, k4.
- Row 7: K4, join yarn to other side of BO, k4.
- Rows 8–29: K every row, working both sides at once.
- Row 30: K4, CO 8, k4.
- Rows 31–35: K.
- BO 16 sts.

Back
- CO 16 sts.
- K 35 rows.
- BO all sts.

Finishing
- With wrong sides together, and starting at top, seam down one side across bottom and up opposite side using running stitch.

Needle Notes: *Making Room for Cords*
When knitting covers for music players, cell phones, or any other hand-held device, keep the gauge loose so that the charger and headphone cords can easily fit through.

✕ ✕ ✕ ✕ ✕ ✕ ✕ ✕ ✕ ✕ ✕ ✕ ✕ ✕ ✕ ✕

Sparkling Water Bottle Holder

Materials
- Needles: straight, size 5 (3¾mm) or size to obtain gauge
- Yarn: 1 hank (50g/108 yds) Tahki Cotton Classic (#3003)

Gauge
16 sts = 4".

Finished Size
Fits a 12–16 oz. water bottle.

Instructions
- CO 5 sts.
- Work in garter stitch until work is 30" long.
- At beginning of next row, CO 27 sts and then 9 sts at beginning of following row. (41 sts)
- K 2 rows.
- Next row begin pattern as follows:
- Row 1 : K1, *yo, k2tog*.
- Row 2: K.
- Row 3 : K1,*K1 wrapping yarn around needle two times*, ending K1.
- Row 4: K.
- Repeat these 4 rows five times, then only Rows 3–4 until holder is as long as desired. For the small bottle featured, repeat Rows 3–4 two more times.

Bottom
- Row 1: K3, *k2tog, k5*.
- Row 2 and every even row: K.
- Row 3: K2,*k2tog, k4*.
- Row 5: K1,*k2tog, k3*.
- Row 7: *K2tog, k2*.
- Row 9: *K2tog*.
- Cut working yarn about 25" long and thread through remaining sts.

Finishing
- Using mattress stitch, seam side and weave in end.
- Sew end of strap to other side of holder and weave in end.

Optional: Weave a strand of brightly colored faux fur yarn in and out of the garter stitch rows to give the water bottle a textured striping effect.

× × × × × × × × × × × × × × × ×

Bubbly Water Bottle Holder

Materials
- Cording or ribbon: 2 yds (for strap)
- Needles: straight, size 11 (8mm) or size to obtain gauge
- Yarn: 1 skein (57g/70 yds) Prism Bubble for yarn A
  1 skein (57g/70 yds) Prism Surf for yarn B

Gauge
16 sts = 4".

Finished Size
Fits a 12–16 oz. water bottle.

Instructions
- CO 11 sts with yarn B.
- Row 1: K.
- Row 2: Increase by kfb each stitch. (22 sts)
- Row 3: K.
- Row 4: K.
- Row 5: K4, kfb, k4, kfb, k4, kfb, k4, kfb, k2. (26 sts)
- Row 6: K.
- Row 7: Add yarn A and knit both yarns together for 5" or to desired length.
- On next row, drop yarn A and continue knitting with only yarn B for 2".
- BO all sts.

Finishing
- Weave in ends.
- Fold BO edge down to Prism Bubble yarn edge and sew to create a casing for the drawstring strap.
- Using mattress stitch, seam side edge from bottom to edge of casing, leaving casing open.
- Draw cording or ribbon through casing and knot. **Note:** Cord is approximately 48" after knotting.

Needle Notes: *Working with Cording*
To save time and avoid having to thread cording through casing, lay cording across work and fold top down over cording while sewing casing down.

X X X X X X X X X X X X X X X X

Fuzzy Pillow

Materials
- Crochet hook: size J (6mm)
- Needles: straight, size 15 (10mm) or size to obtain gauge
- Pillow insert: 12" square
- Yarn: 1 skein (198g/364 yds) Lion Brand Super Saver (Bikini)
  2 skeins (50g/71 yds) Bernat Boa (#81605 Tweety Bird)

Gauge
8 sts = 4".

Finished Size
12" square.

Instructions
- Holding one strand of each yarn together as one, CO 25 sts.
- Work in st st for 38 rows.
- BO all sts.
- Make a second square.

Finishing
- Weave in all ends.
- Line up both knitted squares with wrong sides together. Using crochet hook, single crochet around three sides of squares to connect them.
- Insert pillow and finish crochet along fourth side to close.

Needle Notes: *Recycling Your Yarn*

Recycled yarn is any yarn previously used. Simply unravel yarn from a previous project (old sweaters you don't wear anymore are great), wrap it into a hank, wash if necessary, roll into a ball, and you have recycled yarn ready to use for a new project.

Chapter 7

Gifts

✗ ✗ ✗ ✗ ✗ ✗ ✗ ✗ ✗ ✗ ✗ ✗ ✗ ✗ ✗

Why keep all this fabulous knitting to yourself? Share your passion with the people you care for. Give your favorite aunt a good reason to throw a tea party by giving her a Thrummed Tea Cozy to show off to her closest friends. As she serves, she can tell them how the thrumming provides extra insulation for the teapot.

For that special man in your life, whether he's your father, your brother, or your best friend, knit our striped Guy's Hat & Scarf set to show him how much you care. As he wraps himself in the knitted fabric, he'll really be wrapping up in your love.

For your very best friends, when it's time to celebrate their birthdays, purchase a journal and write a personal note on the first page, then wrap it in a Journal Cover that is knit in their favorite color. They'll be reminded each time they put their feelings down on paper how much they mean to you.

And for family members who are welcoming a new baby, our Baby Blanket is the perfect gift. It is worked on large needles in a super-soft bulky weight yarn and has small eyelets around the edges for weaving a satin ribbon through. Fit for a prince or princess, this is one shower gift that will be cherished for years to come.

Guy's Hat & Scarf

Guy's Hat

Materials
- Needles: circular, size 8 (5mm) or size to obtain gauge
  double-pointed, size 8 (5mm)
  tapestry
- Stitch markers
- Yarn: 100 yards Plymouth Encore Worsted (Cranberry)
  100 yards Plymouth Encore Worsted (Dark Gray)

Gauge
17 sts = 4" in k1 p1 rib
when slightly stretched.

Finished Size
Completed hat will fit head circumference of 22"–24".

Instructions
Note: Change from circular needle to double-pointed needles when there becomes too few sts to complete rnds on the circular needle.
- CO 100 sts with Dark Gray.
- Join sts in the round.
- Place marker to indicate beginning of round.
- Work 3 rnds in k1 p1 rib in Dark Gray.
- Change to Cranberry and work 3 rounds.
- Change to Dark Gray and work 3 rounds.
- Continue switching back and forth between Cranberry and Dark Gray for 3 rounds each for remainder of hat. Work even until hat measures 8" from CO edge.

Decrease for Top of Hat
- Next Rnd: *Work 8 sts in k1 p1 rib, k2tog,* repeat to end of round. (90 sts)
- Next Rnd: *Work 7 sts in k1 p1 rib,

Needle Notes: *Organizing Yarns*

To keep yarns organized and to help avoid tangles especially when using multiple yarns, as for striping, try one of the following: punch holes through one side of a photo box, place the yarn balls inside the box, and thread the strands through the holes; place each ball or skein inside a large plastic zippered baggie with the zipper mostly closed; or place each ball or skein inside a large jar.

k2tog,* repeat to end of round. (80 sts)
- Next Rnd: *Work 6 sts in k1 p1 rib, k2tog,* repeat to end of round. (70 sts)
- Next Rnd: *Work 5 sts in k1 p1 rib, k2tog,* repeat to end of round. (60 sts)
- Next Rnd: *Work 4 sts in k1 p1 rib, k2tog,* repeat to end of round. (50 sts)
- Next Rnd: *Work 3 sts in k1 p1 rib, k2tog,* repeat to end of round. (40 sts)
- Next Rnd: *Work 2 sts in k1 p1 rib, k2tog,* repeat to end of round. (30 sts)

- Next Rnd: *K2tog,* repeat to end of round. (15 sts)
- Next Rnd: K1, *k2tog,* repeat to end of round. (8 sts)

Finishing
- Cut yarn, leaving 24" tail. Thread tail on tapestry needle, draw through remaining sts and pull tight.
- Sew back seam, matching all color changes.
- Weave in all ends.

Guy's Scarf

Materials
- Needles: straight, size 11 (8mm)
- Yarn: 2 balls (100g/200 yds) Plymouth Encore Worsted (Cranberry)
  2 balls (100g/200 yds) Plymouth Encore Worsted (Dark Gray)

Gauge
Not important.

Finished Size
7½" x 72".

Instructions
Note: Work yarn doubled throughout.
- With double strand of Cranberry, CO 36 sts.
- Work in k1 p1 rib for 15 rows.
- Cut yarn and change to a double strand of Dark Gray.
- Work 15 rows.
- Continue alternating Cranberry and Dark Gray, working 15 rows of each, until 19 stripes have been completed, ending with Cranberry stripe.
- BO all sts in rib.
- Weave in all ends.

Needle Notes: *Customizing a Project*

The more you knit, the more comfortable you will become with the supplies and stitch techniques that are used to create all these stylish projects. Soon you will begin to realize that the design possibilities for knitting are almost endless. You can change almost any pattern to reflect your own creativity by adjusting its length or width, adding or deleting a stitch pattern, changing the gauge and needle size, using a different color or more colors, trying a different yarn texture, or adding fringe or other embellishments. These creative decisions can be planned out in advance or made as you knit along.

Journal Cover

Materials
- Button: glass flower
- Needles: straight, size 8 (5mm) or size to obtain gauge
  tapestry
- Sewing needle and thread
- Yarn: 1 skein (50g/122 yds) Debbie Bliss Wool Cotton (#602)
  1 skein (50g/99 yds) GGH Capri (#22)

Gauge
14 sts and 22 rows = 4" .

Finished Size
7" x 15½" to fit 5" x 7" book.

Instructions
- Working both yarns together, CO 60 sts.
- Work in st st for 7".
- BO all sts.

Finishing
- Weave in ends, then iron flat.
- Center your open book on fabric and fold fabric ends over each side of cover. **Note:** The piece should fold over 2" on each end.
- Stretch out fabric if necessary and pin sides at top and bottom edges, creating two pockets on either end for cover of book to slide into.
- Using tapestry needle, sew pocket edges with mattress stitch.

Flower Closure
- Choose one of your yarns and CO 42 sts.
- K first row.
- Row 2: K2, *k1, sl st to left needle, lift next 5 sts over and off end of needle, k slipped st again, k2, repeat from * to end of row.
- Rows 3 and 5: P.
- Row 4 and 6: K1, *k2tog, repeat from * to end.
- Break yarn and thread tail through remaining sts and tie off.
- Center and attach button in flower, using needle and thread.
- Cut 12½" piece of one of your yarns and braid it.
- Loop braid through one of center sts on back of your piece and tie off, creating loop to slip around flower and close over journal cover.

Baby Blanket

Materials

- Needles: straight, size 17 (12¾mm) or size to obtain gauge
- Satin ribbon (optional)
- Yarn: 6 skeins (50g/47 yds) Muench Big Baby

Gauge

8 sts and 5 rows = 4" in st st.

Finished Size

20" x 27".

Instructions

- CO 50 sts.
- Rows 1–3: K in garter stitch.
- Row 4: K3, yo, k2tog, k to last 5 sts, k2tog, yo, k3.
- Row 5: K3, yo, p2tog, k to last 5 sts, p2tog, yo, k3.
- Repeat Rows 4–5 until blanket measures desired length.
- Repeat Rows 1–3.
- BO all sts.
- Weave in ends.

  Optional: Weave satin ribbon through eyelets on both sides if desired.

Great Idea! Knit to Give

Consider donating knitted items to charity. Many charitable organizations accept scarves, hats, blankets, socks, sweaters, and more to give to premature infants, cancer patients, battered women, children who have been separated from their families, teenage mothers, homeless people, elderly people, and others in need.

Thrummed Tea Cozy

Materials
- Needles: double-pointed, size 8 (5mm)
  straight, size 8 (5mm) or size to obtain gauge
  tapestry needle
- Yarn: 1 skein (100g/132 yds) Cascade Pastaza (#1017)
  1½ oz. roving or fleece

Gauge
17 sts and 22 rows = 4".

Finished Size
10½" x 6½".

Instructions

Thrum Technique
Work the thrum by positioning a 3" piece of roving at the back of the work. Insert right needle in stitch below first stitch on left needle. Place roving around needle and pull through then knit stitch on left needle. Pull thrum over this stitch. Drop that piece of roving, knit the required number of stitches, and position the next piece of roving at the back of the work. When the pattern is complete, the right side will have an embroidered look. Meanwhile, the roving ends will be hanging loose on the wrong side of the fabric, providing extra insulation for your tea cozy.

Side I
- CO 40 sts.
- Work in k2 p2 rib for 4 rows.
- **Row 1: K.
- Row 2: P.
- Row 3: *K3, Thrum 1*, repeat from * to * until last 4 sts, k4.
- Row 4: P.
- Row 5: K.
- Row 6: P.
- Row 7: K1,* Thrum 1, k3*, repeat from * to * until last 3 sts, Thrum 1, k2.
- Rows 8: P**.
- Repeat from ** to ** twice.

Decrease
- K2tog, k3 to end. (32 sts)
- P across row.
- K2tog, k2 to end. (24 sts)
- P across row.
- K2tog, k1 to end. (16 sts)
- P across row.
- K2tog to end. (8 sts)
- Thread working yarn onto a tapestry needle, draw through remaining sts and secure.
- Make a second side.

Finishing
- Using the mattress stitch seam sides together for 2" at top and bottom, leaving openings for the handle and spout.

I-cord Tab Top
- CO 5 sts on one double-pointed needle.
- K5, push sts to opposite end of needle, and k.
- Repeat for 5".
- BO sts, leaving a tail.
- Thread tail on a tapestry needle and sew tab to top of tea cozy.

Acknowledgments

A special thanks to the following contributors:

Georgia Coleman
Julianna Danner
Nancy Elkins
Cindy Hartman
Alexis Lantz
Aimee Lavigne
Lulu Macavinta
Mary McCulloch
Cheri McIntyre
Judy McNeil
Liz Miller
Kristal Moffett
Clara Ring
Beate Shambaugh
Lisa Triebwasser
Charlotte Winslow
Janice Yamamoto

Models

Lauren Crockett
Shailey Lewis

Where to Find It

Black Sheep Knittery
Hollywood, CA
www.blacksheepknittery.com

Strands & Stitches
Laguna Beach, CA
www.strandsandstitches.com

Yarn Lady
Laguna Hills, CA
www.yarnlady.com

Book Designer

Deborah Kehoe
Kehoe + Kehoe Design Associates, Inc.,
Burlington, VT

Photographer

Zac Williams

Metric Equivalency Charts

inches to millimeters and centimeters
(mm-millimeters, cm-centimeters)

inches	mm	cm	inches	cm	inches	cm
⅛	3	0.3	9	22.9	30	76.2
¼	6	0.6	10	25.4	31	78.7
½	13	1.3	12	30.5	33	83.8
⅝	16	1.6	13	33.0	34	86.4
¾	19	1.9	14	35.6	35	88.9
⅞	22	2.2	15	38.1	36	91.4
1	25	2.5	16	40.6	37	94.0
1¼	32	3.2	17	43.2	38	96.5
1½	38	3.8	18	45.7	39	99.1
1¾	44	4.4	19	48.3	40	101.6
2	51	5.1	20	50.8	41	104.1
2½	64	6.4	21	53.3	42	106.7
3	76	7.6	22	55.9	43	109.2
3½	89	8.9	23	58.4	44	111.8
4	102	10.2	24	61.0	45	114.3
4½	114	11.4	25	63.5	46	116.8
5	127	12.7	26	66.0	47	119.4
6	152	15.2	27	68.6	48	121.9
7	178	17.8	28	71.1	49	124.5
8	203	20.3	29	73.7	50	127.0

yards to meters

yards	meters	yards	meters	yards	meters	yards	meters	yards	meters
⅛	0.11	2⅛	1.94	4⅛	3.77	6⅛	5.60	8⅛	7.43
¼	0.23	2¼	2.06	4¼	3.89	6¼	5.72	8¼	7.54
⅜	0.34	2⅜	2.17	4⅜	4.00	6⅜	5.83	8⅜	7.66
½	0.46	2½	2.29	4½	4.11	6½	5.94	8½	7.77
⅝	0.57	2⅝	2.40	4⅝	4.23	6⅝	6.06	8⅝	7.89
¾	0.69	2¾	2.51	4¾	4.34	6¾	6.17	8¾	8.00
⅞	0.80	2⅞	2.63	4⅞	4.46	6⅞	6.29	8⅞	8.12
1	0.91	3	2.74	5	4.57	7	6.40	9	8.23
1⅛	1.03	3⅛	2.86	5⅛	4.69	7⅛	6.52	9⅛	8.34
1¼	1.14	3¼	2.97	5¼	4.80	7¼	6.63	9¼	8.46
1⅜	1.26	3⅜	3.09	5⅜	4.91	7⅜	6.74	9⅜	8.57
1½	1.37	3½	3.20	5½	5.03	7½	6.86	9½	8.69
1⅝	1.49	3⅝	3.31	5⅝	5.14	7⅝	6.97	9⅝	8.80
1¾	1.60	3¾	3.43	5¾	5.26	7¾	7.09	9¾	8.92
1⅞	1.71	3⅞	3.54	5⅞	5.37	7⅞	7.20	9⅞	9.03
2	1.83	4	3.66	6	5.49	8	7.32	10	9.14

Index

A

Abbreviations 11
Accessories 112
Adding Embellishments 95
Allow for Stretch 85
Arm Warmers 84
Ask for Help 17

B

Baby Blanket 130
Bag with Pom-Poms 98
Basic Techniques 13
Beanie Cap 70
Belts & Caps 62
Biggy Rib Scarf 36
Bind Off 18
Blocking Pins 11
Bubbly Water Bottle Holder 118

C

Cable Needles 10
Caring for Your Needles 27
Cast On 14
Changing Yarns 23
Check Your Work 73
Choosing a Knitting Bag 41
Clutch Purse 102
Colinette Shrug 58
Combining Colors & Textures 8
Continuous Shrug 52
Contributors 134
Copy Your Pattern 39
Correcting Too Many Stitches 59
Crochet 25
Crochet Hooks 11
Cuirass Shrug 56
Customizing a Project 127

E

Evening Bag 100

F

Fall Belt 72
Felted Mini Purse 94
Felted Purse 90
Felted Purse with Handles 96
Felted Tigress Bag 92
Felting 31
Finishing & Seaming 26

Fringe 32
Fun in Numbers 19
Fuzzy Bunny Scarf 38
Fuzzy Pillow 120

G

Garter Stitch 17
Gauge 12
Gauge Ruler/Needle Sizer 10
Gently Unravel Rows 29
Gifts 122
Guy's Hat & Scarf 124

H

Hand Warmers 86
Headband Scarf 48
Holding a Needle & Yarn 15

I

I-Cord 33
I-Pod Cozy 114
Identifying Resilient Yarns 87
Island Poncho 54

J

Jot Down the Details 65
Journal Cover 128

K

Karaoke Felted Purse 106
Knit Stitch 16
Knit to Give 131
Knitting in the Round 24
Knitting Needles 9
Knitting Supplies 7

L

Lining Your Handbag 111

M

Making a Slip Knot 13
Making Room for Cords 115
Mixing Your Yarns 14

N

Needle Sizes 14

O

Organizing Yarns 125

P

Point Protectors 11
Pom-Pom 33

Purl Stitch 16
Purses & Handbags 88

R

Reading a Knitting Pattern 53
Reading a Yarn Label 45
Recycled Yarn Bag 104
Recycling Your Yarn 121
Reinforcing the Soles 79
Relax the Tension 57
Retro Checkered Scarf 42
Reverse Stockinette Stitch 17
Ribbing 18
Row Counters 10

S

Scarves 34
Shaping 19
Shrugs & Ponchos 50
Skelt Scarf 40
Slippers 76
Softee Scarf 44
Sparkling Purse 110
Sparkling Water Bottle Holder 116
Stitch Holders 10
Stitch Markers 10
Stockinette Stitch 17
Summer Shrug 60

T

Tapestry Needle 10
Tassel 32
Teen's Hat 66
Thrummed Tea Cozy 132
Tips for Left-Handed Knitters 37
Trendsetter Belt 64
Tube Top/Skirt 82

U

Using Circular Needles 67
Using Different Needles 69

W

Warmies 74
Working with Cording 119
Woven "Braid" Scarf 46
Wrist Warmers 80

Y

Yarns 7

✗ ✗ ✗ ✗ ✗ ✗ ✗ ✗ ✗ ✗